CHILDREN'S
WORLD ATLAS

Claudia Martin

ARCTURUS

ARCTURUS

This edition published in 2021 by Arcturus Publishing Limited
26/27 Bickels Yard, 151–153 Bermondsey Street,
London SE1 3HA

Author: Claudia Martin
Designer: Lorraine Inglis
Editor: Becca Clunes
Picture research: Paul Futcher and Lorraine Inglis
Cartography: Lovell Johns
Consultant: Philip Steele
Managing Editor: Joe Harris

In this book, one billion means one thousand million (1,000,000,000) and one trillion means one million million (1,000,000,000,000).

ISBN: 978-1-83857-639-4
CH007399NT
Supplier 42, Date 0521, Print run 11280

Printed in Singapore

CHILDREN'S
WORLD ATLAS

CONTENTS

The World

Earth is around 149 million km (93 million miles) from the Sun, where it is warmed just the right amount for rain to fall, plants to grow, and animals to live. From steamy rainforests to the frozen poles, from rocky islands to towering cities, our planet is home to nearly 8 billion people, as well as many trillions of animals and plants.

Continents

People usually divide Earth's land into seven continents. These are large expanses of land that are often separated from each other by water. From largest to smallest, the continents are: Asia, Africa, North America, South America, Antarctica, Europe, and Australia.

NORTH AMERICA

ATLANTIC OCEAN

PACIFIC OCEAN

The American landmass is divided into two continents at one of its narrowest points.

SOUTH AMERICA

Not everyone agrees on the dividing line between Europe and Asia, but many people say it is the Ural Mountains, which run through Russia.

Oceans

Ocean covers 71 perent of Earth's surface. People usually divide the world ocean into five. From largest to smallest, the five oceans are the Pacific, Atlantic, Indian, Southern, and Arctic. Seas are large areas of saltwater that are partly or fully surrounded by land.

Ocean islands are often said to be part of the nearest continent. The Maldives in the Indian Ocean are part of Asia.

Countries

People have divided the world into 195 countries with agreed borders. Each country has its own government, as well as a capital city or cities, where the government works. Some islands or areas are part of countries that lie thousands of miles away. Antarctica is the largest area that is not part of any country.

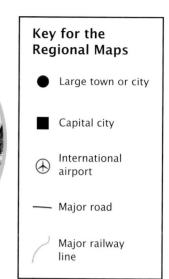

With an area of 0.44 sq km (0.17 sq miles), the smallest country is Vatican City, which is ruled by the head of the Catholic Church, the Pope.

Key for the Regional Maps

● Large town or city

■ Capital city

⊕ International airport

— Major road

Major railway line

ARCTIC OCEAN

ASIA

EUROPE

PACIFIC OCEAN

AFRICA

The Australian continent is often grouped with islands in the Pacific Ocean into a region called Oceania.

INDIAN OCEAN

AUSTRALIA

SOUTHERN OCEAN

ANTARCTICA

DID YOU KNOW? The continents have not always looked as they do today, due to the constant slow movement of the giant plates of rock, called tectonic plates, that lie beneath them.

Populations

The world's population is growing because, every year, more people are born than die. In 1900, there were 1.6 billion people in the world. By 2000 there were 6 billion people. By 2024, the population will pass 8 billion. The world's population is not evenly spread across its countries, or even within countries. People usually cluster where there is plenty of work, in busy cities or on good farmland.

Largest Population

The country with the largest population is China, with 1.4 billion inhabitants. This large population is due to China's vast area, with much of its land perfect for growing crops over many thousands of years. The country that is most densely populated, or crowded with people, is Monaco, in Europe, which has an area of just 2 sq km (0.78 sq miles). Monaco has 19,000 inhabitants per sq km (49,000 per sq mile).

Every year, the narrow, twisting roads of Monaco are used for the Grand Prix motor race.

Smallest Population

The country with the smallest population is also the smallest country: Vatican City, which has around 1,000 inhabitants. The least densely populated island is Greenland, a part of Denmark. The world's largest island, Greenland is home to 0.03 people per sq km (0.08 per sq mile). Three-quarters of Greenland's land is covered by ice.

Greenland has a population of around 57,000.

DID YOU KNOW? Due to better medical care and diet, the number of people aged 80 or over is expected to increase from around 143 million today to over 900 million by 2100.

Growing and Shrinking

Many countries, such as Niger in Africa, have quickly growing populations. This happens when the number of deaths per year is low because of better medicine and farming methods. Alongside this, many families have more than two children. Some countries, such as Bahrain in Asia, have growing populations because many people move there to work. A few countries have shrinking populations because families have fewer children and many people move abroad to work.

The population of Lithuania, in Eastern Europe, shrank from 3.7 million in 1990 to 2.8 million today.

Arctic regions are among the least densely populated places on Earth.

Population Density

This map shows how population is spread across the world.

Up to 3 people per 1 sq km (0.4 sq miles)

Up to 100 people per 1 sq km (0.4 sq miles)

Up to 20,000 people per 1 sq km (0.4 sq miles)

Bangladesh is one of the most densely populated countries in Asia.

LARGEST CITIES

Tokyo, Japan: 38.5 million people
Jakarta, Indonesia: 30 million people
Seoul, South Korea: 25.5 million people
Manila, Philippines: 24.1 million people
New York, United States: 23.7 million people
Shanghai, China: 23.4 million people
Cairo, Egypt: 22.4 million people

Shanghai

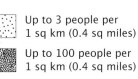

Languages

There are between 6,000 and 7,000 languages spoken around the world. Many languages are spoken in just one region, while others have been spread across the world as people conquered or settled in other places. Most countries have one or more official languages, which are widely spoken and used by their government.

Common Languages

More people speak Mandarin Chinese as their first language (the language they learn from their parents) than any other language: 918 million. Other languages widely spoken as a first language are: Spanish (460 million), English (379 million), Hindi (341 million), and Arabic (315 million). The world's most widely understood language is English, as 1.5 billion people have learned it at home or in school.

Chinese is spoken wherever Chinese people have settled. These Chinese Canadians are celebrating Chinese New Year in Vancouver, Canada.

Spanish was brought to the Americas by settlers after 1492.

Endangered Languages

An endangered language is one that may soon fall out of use. This happens because all the speakers of the language either die or swap to another, more common, language. Endangered languages include many spoken by Native Americans, Aboriginal Australians, and other indigenous peoples, who were the first inhabitants of a region.

There are only 150 speakers of the Tsuut'ina language, spoken by the Tsuut'ina Nation of Alberta, Canada. This Tsuut'ina man is wearing traditional clothes for a celebration.

DID YOU KNOW? Half the world's population speak one of just 23 common languages, while over 2,800 languages are endangered, many of them with fewer than 1,000 speakers.

COUNTRIES WITH MOST LANGUAGES
(AND THEIR MOST SPOKEN LANGUAGES)

Papua New Guinea: 840, including Enga and Melpa
Indonesia: 710, including Indonesian and Javanese
Nigeria: 524, including Hausa and English
India: 453, including Hindi and English
United States: 335, including English and Spanish
Australia: 319, including English and Mandarin Chinese
China: 305, including Mandarin and Yue Chinese

A traditional gathering, called a sing-sing, in Papua New Guinea

Mandarin Chinese is an official language only in China and Singapore.

Official Languages

This map shows the countries that have one of the world's most common languages as an official or national language.

Mandarin Chinese

English

Hindi-Urdu

Spanish

Arabic

New Zealand is one of over 60 countries with English as an official language.

Industries

People work in many industries, from mining to making movies. Experts often put industries into three groups: those that use the land or sea, those that make products to sell, and those that offer services. Experts also put countries into groups, depending on their wealth and range of industries: "least developed," "developing," and "developed." In a "least developed" country, many people live in poverty.

Using the Land and Sea

Industries that collect natural resources are called primary industries. They include farming, fishing, hunting, mining for metals or fuels, and cutting down trees. In "least developed" countries, many people work in primary industries.

Farmers keep animals or grow crops. Crops are used for food, oil, cloth-making, or even toiletries, like this French lavender.

Products and Services

Industries that turn natural resources into products are called secondary industries. They turn tomatoes into soup, metal into cars, and wood into furniture. Industries that provide services to people are called tertiary industries. Services include entertainment, transport, healthcare, teaching, and banking. In "developed" countries, many people are employed in services, while the primary and secondary industries often use machines instead of human workers.

These workers are manufacturing mobile phones in a factory in Bangladesh.

LARGEST CROPS
(AND THE COUNTRIES WITH THE BIGGEST HARVEST)

Sugarcane: Brazil
Maize, also called corn: United States
Rice: China
Wheat: China
Potatoes: China
Soya beans: United States
Cassava: Nigeria

Growing best in warm regions, sugarcane is used to make sugar as well as ethanol, which can be burned in car engines as a cleaner choice than petrol.

Mongolia does not have a wide enough range of industries to be called a "developed" country.

Japan is one of the world's most "developed" countries.

Afghanistan is a "least developed" country because long wars have destroyed its industries.

Industrial Development

This map divides countries into three levels of development. "Developed" countries are wealthy and have a wide range of industries.

- Least developed
- Developed
- Developing

DID YOU KNOW? In the United Kingdom, the use of farming machinery means that only 1 percent of adults work in farming, while in Burundi, in Africa, around 90 percent of adults are farmers.

Biomes

A biome is an area where a particular group of plants and animals live, all of them well suited to the climate. Biomes range from deserts to rainforests. A region's climate is its usual temperature and rainfall. Climate depends on distance from the equator, where the Sun is hottest, and features of the landscape, such as mountains.

Polar Ice

This is the world's coldest biome, with the temperature usually below 0°C (32°F). With the land covered by ice, no plants can survive. Only a few animals live in this biome, including polar bears and penguins.

Tundra

In far northern regions, just to the south of the polar ice, it is too cold for trees to grow. Grasses, mosses, and low shrubs take root in partly frozen soil. Animals often have thick fur or feathers to stay warm.

Mountain

On high mountain slopes, trees cannot survive the cold and wind. There are only grasses and other low plants, along with sure-footed animals such as mountain goats. Snow covers the tallest summits.

Coniferous Forest

Coniferous forests are home to trees with needle-shaped leaves, such as pines and firs. These trees do not lose their leaves in winter. Coniferous forests form a band across the world's cool northern regions.

The mountain biome stretches through the Andes Mountains in South America.

Deciduous Forest

This biome has many deciduous trees, which lose their broad, flat leaves in winter. Deciduous forests are common in temperate regions, which lie between the hot tropics and the cold poles.

Tropical Rain Forest

Tropical rain forests are in hot regions with lots of rain. In this climate, trees grow tall, and many smaller plants live beneath. Rain forests are home to half of all plant and animal species, including sloths.

Mediterranean

This biome is found around the Mediterranean Sea, as well as other regions with hot, dry summers and rainy winters. Although shrubs cover much of the land, grassland and forest are also common.

DID YOU KNOW? All the world's biomes are at risk from expanding cities and farmland; activities such as mining and cutting down trees; and pollution.

LARGEST DESERTS

Antarctica: 14 million sq km (5.5 million sq miles)

Sahara Desert: 9.2 million sq km (3.6 million sq miles); northern Africa

Arabian Desert: 2.3 million sq km (900,000 sq miles); western Asia

Gobi Desert: 1.3 million sq km (500,000 sq miles); eastern Asia

Kalahari Desert: 900,000 sq km (350,000 sq miles); southern Africa

Arabian Desert

Russia is the country with the most trees, around 642 billion, many of them in the vast northern coniferous forests.

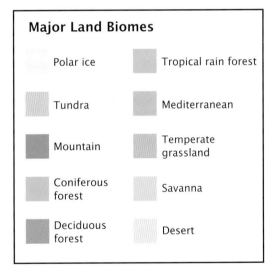

Major Land Biomes

Polar ice	Tropical rain forest
Tundra	Mediterranean
Mountain	Temperate grassland
Coniferous forest	Savanna
Deciduous forest	Desert

Temperate Grassland

Most plants in temperate grassland are grasses or shrubs. Moderate temperatures and rainfall make many grassland areas suited to growing crops, so wide areas that were once grassland are now farmland.

Savanna

Savanna is found in tropical regions where there is a dry season and a rainy season. Savanna is grassland with scattered bushes and trees. Herds of grass- and plant-eaters, such as giraffes, roam the land.

Desert

A desert is an area with so little rain that few plants and animals can survive. Deserts can be in hot or cold regions. Lack of rain is caused by hot, dry air; extreme cold; or factors such as distance from the sea.

Africa

Africa is the second largest continent, after Asia. It makes up one-fifth of the world's land. There are 54 countries in Africa, home to over 1.3 billion people. Africa's most southerly point is Cape Agulhas, in South Africa. Its most northerly point is Cape Angela, in Tunisia.

The Sahara Desert

The Sahara Desert covers more than 9 million sq km (3.6 million sq miles) of North Africa. It is the world's largest hot desert. Most of the desert's surface is bare rock, a type of desert landscape called hamada. Some regions are covered by sand dunes, reaching over 180 m (590 ft) high.

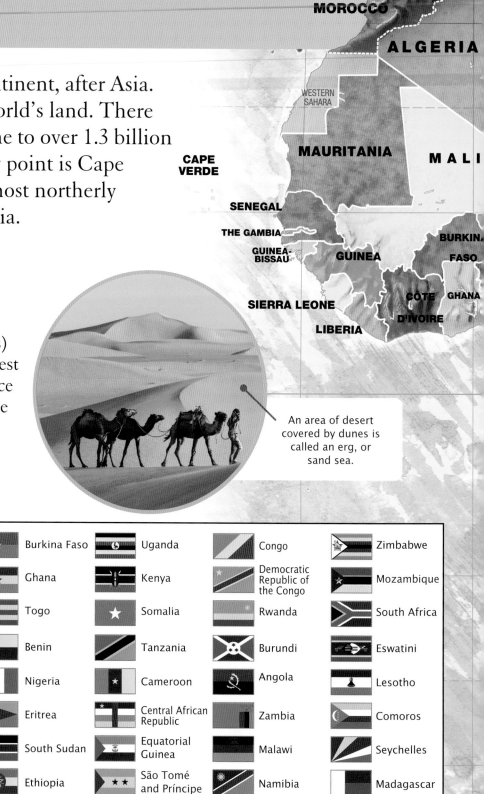

MOROCCO

ALGERIA

WESTERN SAHARA

CAPE VERDE

MAURITANIA

MALI

SENEGAL

THE GAMBIA

GUINEA-BISSAU

GUINEA

BURKINA FASO

CÔTE D'IVOIRE

GHANA

SIERRA LEONE

LIBERIA

An area of desert covered by dunes is called an erg, or sand sea.

	Egypt		Sudan		Burkina Faso		Uganda		Congo		Zimbabwe
	Morocco		Cape Verde		Ghana		Kenya		Democratic Republic of the Congo		Mozambique
	Algeria		Senegal		Togo		Somalia		Rwanda		South Africa
	Tunisia		Gambia		Benin		Tanzania		Burundi		Eswatini
	Libya		Guinea–Bissau		Nigeria		Cameroon		Angola		Lesotho
	Mauritania		Guinea		Eritrea		Central African Republic		Zambia		Comoros
	Mali		Sierra Leone		South Sudan		Equatorial Guinea		Malawi		Seychelles
	Niger		Liberia		Ethiopia		São Tomé and Príncipe		Namibia		Madagascar
	Chad		Côte d'Ivoire		Djibouti		Gabon		Botswana		Mauritius

DID YOU KNOW? Africa is the continent with the youngest population. Its average age is 19, while the average age of all the other continents is 30.

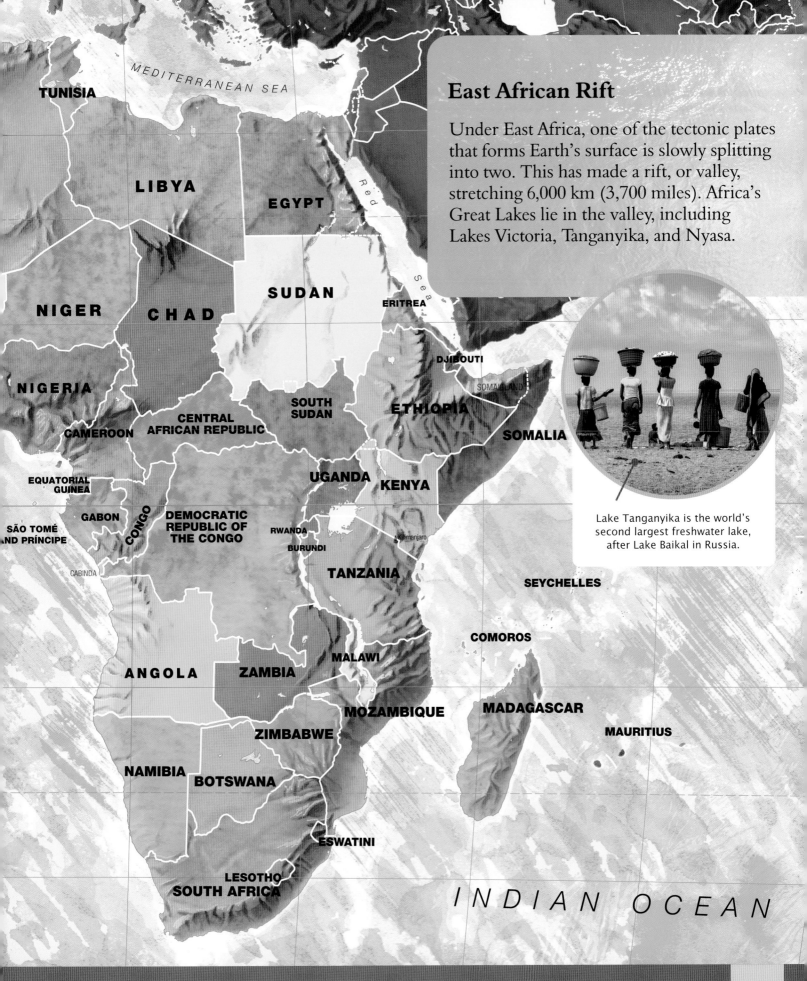

MEDITERRANEAN SEA

TUNISIA

LIBYA

EGYPT

Red Sea

NIGER

CHAD

SUDAN

ERITREA

NIGERIA

DJIBOUTI

SOMALILAND

SOUTH
SUDAN

ETHIOPIA

CAMEROON

CENTRAL
AFRICAN REPUBLIC

SOMALIA

EQUATORIAL
GUINEA

UGANDA

KENYA

GABON

CONGO

DEMOCRATIC
REPUBLIC OF
THE CONGO

RWANDA

Kilimanjaro

SÃO TOMÉ
AND PRÍNCIPE

BURUNDI

CABINDA

TANZANIA

SEYCHELLES

COMOROS

MALAWI

ANGOLA

ZAMBIA

MOZAMBIQUE

MADAGASCAR

MAURITIUS

ZIMBABWE

NAMIBIA

BOTSWANA

ESWATINI

LESOTHO

SOUTH AFRICA

INDIAN OCEAN

East African Rift

Under East Africa, one of the tectonic plates that forms Earth's surface is slowly splitting into two. This has made a rift, or valley, stretching 6,000 km (3,700 miles). Africa's Great Lakes lie in the valley, including Lakes Victoria, Tanganyika, and Nyasa.

Lake Tanganyika is the world's second largest freshwater lake, after Lake Baikal in Russia.

Egypt

Egypt is among Africa's wealthiest countries, earning much of its money from oil, mining, and tourism. More than 14 million tourists arrive every year to visit Egypt's many ancient sites. Around 90 percent of Egyptians are Muslims, while most of the rest are Christians.

Pyramids

In around 3100 BCE, Egypt was united under one ruler, or pharaoh. For the next 3,000 years, Egypt was home to a great civilization. When a pharaoh died, their body was placed in a tomb, surrounded by precious objects for use in the afterlife. From 2630 BCE to 1550 BCE, pharaohs' tombs were in stone pyramids. The largest was the Pyramid of Khufu, at Giza, which took around 20 years to build from 2.3 million blocks of limestone and granite.

There are three main pyramids at Giza, built for (front to back) Pharaohs Menkaure, Khafre, and Khufu, as well as smaller pyramids for queens.

At about 6,650 km (4,130 miles) long, the Nile is Africa's longest river.

The Nile River

The Nile flows through 11 countries in northeastern Africa, before emptying into the Mediterranean Sea in northern Egypt. The river has always been Egypt's greatest source of water, giving life to crops with its yearly floods over the surrounding land. Since 1970, the Aswan High Dam, in southern Egypt, has controlled the flooding and stored water for use in dry periods.

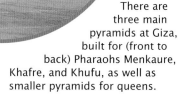

The temples at Abu Simbel were carved from the mountainside to celebrate a battle won by Pharaoh Ramesses II in 1274 BCE.

DID YOU KNOW? Egypt's Sinai Peninsula is in Asia, divided from Africa and the rest of Egypt by the Gulf of Suez and the humanmade Suez Canal.

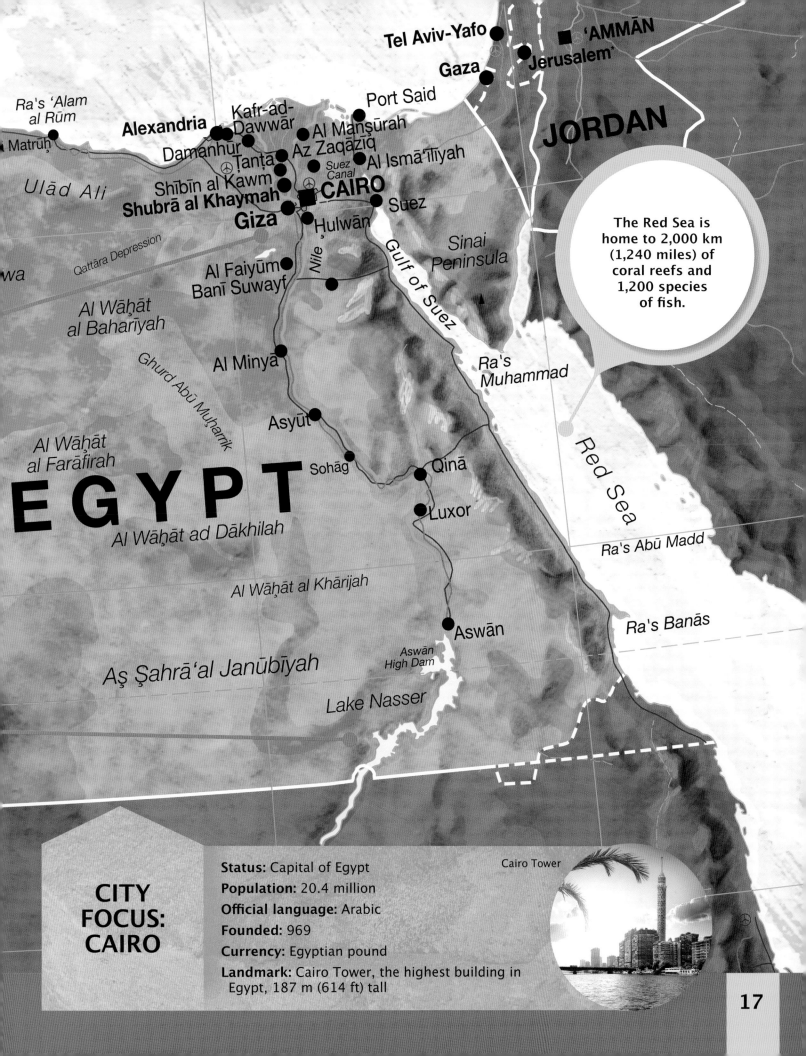

Ra's 'Alam al Rūm

Matrūḥ

Alexandria

Kafr-ad-Dawwār

Damanhūr

Ulād Ali

wa

Qattāra Depression

Port Said

Al Manṣūrah

Az Zaqāzīq

Ṭanṭa

Suez Canal

Al Ismā'īliyah

Shībīn al Kawm

Shubrā al Khaymah

CAIRO

Giza

Ḥulwān

Suez

Tel Aviv-Yafo

Gaza

Jerusalem*

■ **'AMMĀN**

JORDAN

Al Faiyūm

Nile

Banī Suwayf

Al Wāḥāt al Bahariyah

Sinai Peninsula

Gulf of Suez

Ra's Muhammad

The Red Sea is home to 2,000 km (1,240 miles) of coral reefs and 1,200 species of fish.

Ghurd Abū Muḥarrik

Al Minyā

Al Wāḥāt al Farāfirah

Asyūṭ

E G Y P T

Sohāg

Qinā

Red Sea

Al Wāḥāt ad Dākhilah

Luxor

Ra's Abū Madd

Al Wāḥāt al Khārijah

Ra's Banās

Aş Ṣahrā' al Janūbīyah

Aswān

Aswān High Dam

Lake Nasser

CITY FOCUS: CAIRO

Status: Capital of Egypt

Population: 20.4 million

Official language: Arabic

Founded: 969

Currency: Egyptian pound

Landmark: Cairo Tower, the highest building in Egypt, 187 m (614 ft) tall

North Africa

Morocco, Algeria, Tunisia, and Libya face the Mediterranean Sea. Green farmland stretches along the coast, but south of the Atlas Mountains is the Sahara Desert. This region has long been home to Berber people. From the 7th century, Arabs from the Middle East settled, bringing their religion (Islam) and language (Arabic).

Madrasas

From its birth in the early 7th century, Islam placed a great value on education, so that every Muslim could read their holy book, the Quran. As Islam spread across North Africa, many schools and universities, called madrasas, were built.

After it was built in 1356, students of all ages learned at the Bou Inania Madrasa in Fès, Morocco.

The *gimbri* is made from wood, camel skin, and goat-gut strings.

Berber Music

Traditionally, the Berber were herders of camels, sheep, and goats. Several styles of music grew up in Berber villages, including music played for dances, music for weddings, and the poems sung by visting musicians. Berber instruments include a large drum (*bendir*), lute (*gimbri*), flute (*ajouag*), and a stringed instrument played with a bow (*rebab*).

The Sahara Desert stretches from the region of Western Sahara to Egypt.

Kénitra
RABAT
Casablanca
Safi
Khen
Marrakech
Cap Rhir
Atlas
Cap Drâa
Oued Drâa
Hamada du Drâa
El Aaíun
(Laâyoune)
Saguia al Hamra
Cap Boujdour
Zemmour
Yetti
Erg Iguidi
El Eglab
Rhallamane
WESTERN
Golfe de Cintra
Karet
El Hammâmi
El Hank
S
SAHARA
Hamâd
Azzeffâl
Erg Atou
Trarza
Aklé Aouâna
Lac de Guier

DID YOU KNOW? With an area of 2,381,740 sq km (919,595 sq miles), Algeria is the largest African country and 5,281 times the size of the smallest, Seychelles.

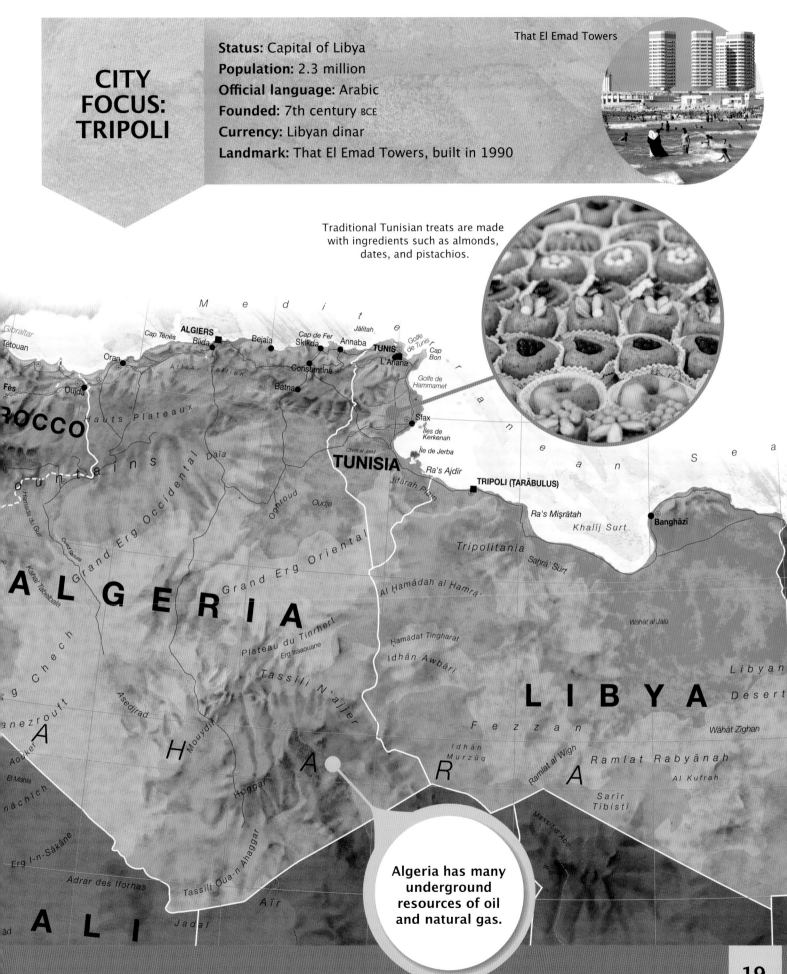

CITY FOCUS: TRIPOLI

Status: Capital of Libya
Population: 2.3 million
Official language: Arabic
Founded: 7th century BCE
Currency: Libyan dinar
Landmark: That El Emad Towers, built in 1990

That El Emad Towers

Traditional Tunisian treats are made with ingredients such as almonds, dates, and pistachios.

Algeria has many underground resources of oil and natural gas.

The Sahel

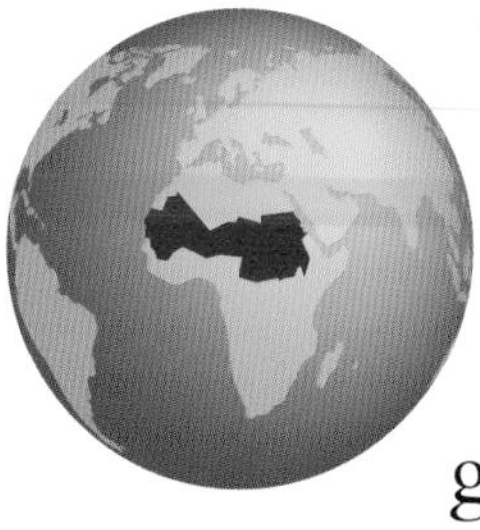

"Sahel" comes from the Arabic word for "coast," because this region borders the sand sea of the Sahara Desert. Not as dry as the Sahara to the north, nor as wet as the savanna to the south, the Sahel is a place of dry grasslands and thorny shrublands. Its countries include Mauritania, Mali, Niger, Chad, and Sudan.

Niger is one of the world's poorest countries, because of droughts and the growing desert.

Mud Bricks

In this region, people started building with mud bricks at least 2,000 years ago. The mud is mixed with water, sand, and straw, shaped into bricks, then baked in the sun. Walls are smoothed with mud plaster. The sticks that support the building's structure are often left sticking out from the walls as decoration. They are also used to climb up when the plaster need replacing.

Everyone in Djenné, in Mali, helps to repair the Great Mosque once a year.

A sandstorm in Khartoum

CITY FOCUS: KHARTOUM

Status: Capital of Sudan

Population: 5.2 million

Official language: Sudanese Arabic and English

Founded: 1821

Currency: Sudanese pound

Landmark: Tuti Bridge, the first suspension bridge in Sudan, completed in 2008

Land at Risk

The Sahara Desert is slowly spreading into the Sahel. Many people are trying to live on the land bordering the desert, grazing their animals and cutting down trees so they can grow crops. This is stripping bare the soil, which is being carried away by wind and rain. Without soil, the land becomes desert, where animals and plants cannot live.

The climate in the Sahel is hot, sunny, and dry.

At Meroë, in Sudan, are more than 200 pyramids, built between 2,700 and 1,700 years ago.

Around 8 out of every 10 people in Chad are farmers.

Map labels

A R A

Plateau du Marigueni

Sarir Tibisti

Massif d'Aïr

Aş Şahrā'al Janūbiyah

Aswān

Ra's Banās

Lake Nasser

Nubian Desert

Ras al Ḥadāribah

Jiddah

Ténéré du Tafassásset

Aïr

Grand Erg de Bilma

al Aḥmar

Port Sudan

Talak

Borkou

Ounianga

Ash Shamālīyah

Barq al Bishārīyīn

Kassala

Erg du Ténéré

Erg du Djourab

Massif Ennedi
Plateau de Basso

Shamāl Dārfūr

S U D A N

N I G E R

Bodélé

Telga Plateau

Omdurman

Al Kharţūm Baḩrī

Zinder

Kanem

Zagaoua

Shamāl Kurdufān

KHARTOUM

Meroë

ASM

Katsina

LAKE CHAD

Dagana

Ghirb Dārfūr

Al. Jazirah

Wad Madanī

Al Qaḑārif

Gusau

Kano

Borno

C H A D

Batha

Al Ubayyid

Zaria

Maiduguri

NDJAMÉNA

Janūb Dārfūr

Janūb Kurdufān

An Nīal Azraq

Kaduna

Maroua

Bauchi

Gombe

Cher

S a l a m a t

N I G E R I A

Logone

B. Aoua

C E N T R A L
A F R I C A N
R E P U B L I C

Northern
Baḩr al Ghazāl

Warrap

S O U T H

S U D A N

Unity

Jonglei

Upper Nile

DID YOU KNOW? One of the richest people of all time was Musa I (c.1280–c.1337), ruler of Mali, because of his empire's many gold and salt mines.

West Africa

Brakna
Aouker
Hodh
Affollè
Lac de Guier
Sénégal
Thiès
DAKAR
Ferlo
SENEGAL
Boundou
THE GAMBIA
BANJUL
Gambia
Ziguinchor
Cap Roxo
Baoulé
Bafing
Niger
BAMAKO
GUINEA-BISSAU
BISSAU
Ilha de Orango
Îles Tristao
GUINEA
Niger
CONAKRY
Îles de Los
FREETOWN
SIERRA LEONE
Sherbro Island
Tienba
Bomi Hills
MONROVIA
LIBERIA
Daloa
Sassandra
Grain Coast
Cape Palmas

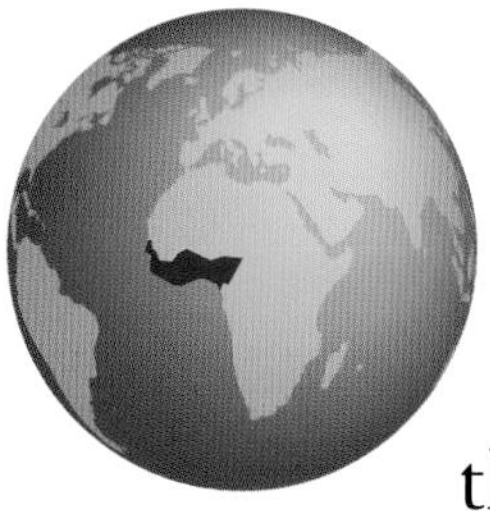

The savanna gives way to forest around the Atlantic Coast. While many West Africans are farmers, the region is also home to quickly growing cities. Nigeria has some of the fastest-growing cities south of the Sahara Desert. Many city-dwellers work in factories that make goods such as textiles and cars.

These griots are singing the family history of a new chief, in Kokemnoure, Burkina Faso.

Griots

Griots are traditional West African musicians. They sing and play instruments, telling histories, stories, and poems passed down from one generation to the next. In the past, griots were so important they were also advisors to kings.

Liberia is home to the world's largest plantation of rubber trees, where rubber is collected for use in tyres and shoes.

CITY FOCUS: ABUJA

Status: Capital of Nigeria
Population: 2.4 million
Official language: English
Founded: 1828
Currency: Naira
Landmark: Nigerian National Mosque, completed in 1984

Nigerian National Mosque

M A L I

ké Aouâna

Azaouàd

Lac
Faguibine

Niger

Lac
Garou
Lac Haribomo
Lac Do
Lac Niangay

Lac Débo

Lac Korarou

Massina

Niger

Mole National
Park, in Ghana, is
home to African
bush elephants,
the largest
land animals.

Nakambé

NIAMEY

Zinder

LAKE
CHAD

BURKINA

Volta

OUAGADOUGOU

Sokoto

Katsina

Gusau

Kano

Borno

Maiduguri

Bobo-Dioulasso

FASO

Gourounsi

Gourma

BENIN

NIGERIA

Zaria

Maroua

Mouhoun

Kainji
Reservoir

Kaduna

Gombe

Tamale

Parakou

Shiroro
Reservoir

Jos

Bauchi
Jos Plateau

Garoua

Akosombo
Dam

ABUJA

Benue

Lac de
Lagdo

GHANA

TOGO

Ilorin

Bénue

LAKE
VOLTA

Ogbomoso
Iseyin Oyo
Ede

Ila Orangun

Vina

Bouaké

Kumasi

Iwo
Ibadan
Abeokuta

Oshogbo
Ife

Ado-Ekiti
Ikere
Owo

Béroui
Bouanoua

RE
YAMOUSSOUKRO

Ashanti

Volta

Ondo

YAMOUSSOUKRO

Mushin
Ikorodu

Benin
City

Enugu

Abidjan
Coast

ACCRA

LOMÉ
Cotonou
PORTO-NOVO
Lagos

Onitsha

Biafra

Cape
Three Points

Gold Coast

Slave Coast

Mouths of the Niger

Warri

Niger

Aba

Port Harcourt

Calabar

Bandama

MALABO

Nigeria is
profiting from its
natural resources,
including oil and
gemstones.

Bioko

Gulf of Guinea

Cocoa trees were
brought to West
Africa from the
Americas in the
19th century.

Cocoa Beans

Cocoa beans are a valuable crop because they are used to
make chocolate. They are the seeds of cocoa trees, which
grow best in a hot, wet climate. More than two-thirds of the
world's cocoa beans are grown in West Africa.

DID YOU KNOW? In Togo, many people follow traditional religious beliefs, known as Animism,
in which all places and animals are believed to have spirits and be central to human life.

East Africa

Due to the movement of tectonic plates, East Africa boasts Africa's lowest point, Lake Assal in Djibouti, and its highest, Mount Kilimanjaro in Tanzania. The region is known for its wildlife, including elephants, leopards, lions, and rhinoceroses, although these animals are all threatened by loss of their habitat.

First Footprints

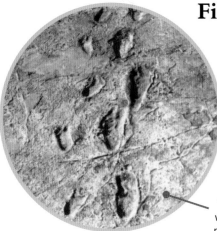

Scientists think that humans are descended from a group of apes that lived in Africa around 7 million years ago. Many fossils of our early ancestors, with features of both apes and humans, have been found in East Africa. In Laetoli, in Tanzania, fossilized footprints show that our ancestors were walking on two legs by at least 3.7 million years ago.

The Laetoli footprints were made by two adults as they walked through damp ash thrown out by a volcano. The prints were baked in the sun, then covered by more ash.

Mount Kilimanjaro

Africa's highest mountain is a volcano, formed by lava that erupted then hardened into rock. Mount Kilimanjaro has not erupted for around 150,000 years.

At 5,895 m (19,341 ft), the peak of Mount Kilimanjaro is covered by ice all year.

CITY FOCUS: NAIROBI

Status: Capital of Kenya

Population: 4.4 million

Official languages: English and Swahili

Founded: 1899

Currency: Kenyan shilling

Landmark: Nairobi National Park, founded in 1946

Zebras in Nairobi National Park

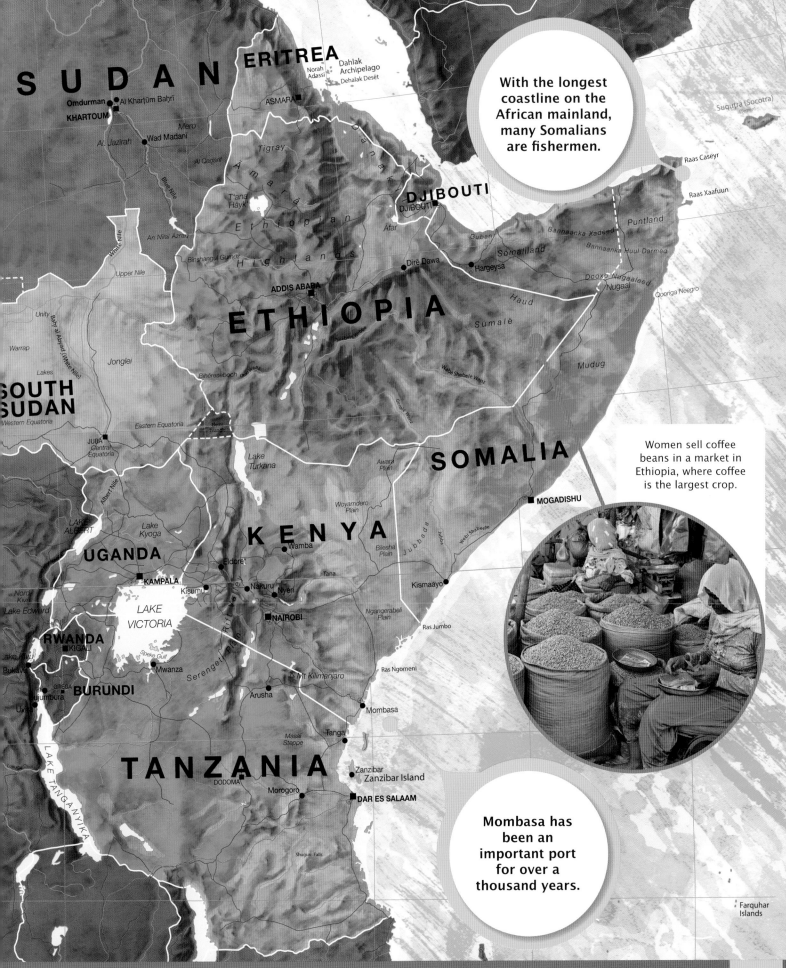

SUDAN

ERITREA

Omdurman • Al Kharṭūm Baḥrī
KHARTOUM

Al Jazirah
Wad Madanī

Merowe

Blue Nile

Tigray

Āmarā

Āmarā

White Nile

An Nīlal Azraq

Upper Nile

Binshangul Gumuz

Ethiopian

Highlands

ADDIS ABABA

ETHIOPIA

T'ana Hāyk'

Norah Adassi

Dahlak Archipelago

Dehalak Desēt

ASMARA

Danakil

DJIBOUTI

DJIBOUTI

Āfar

Dirē Dawa

Guban

Hargeysa

Somaliland

Banaanka Xadeed

Bannaanka Huul Darmed

Puntland

Dooxo Nugaaleed

Nugaal

Qooriga Neegro

Suquṭra (Socotra)
(Yemen)

Raas Caseyr

Raas Xaafuun

Haud

Sumalē

Wabē Shebelē Wenz

Mudug

SOUTH
SUDAN

Western Equatoria

Warrap

Unity

Bahr al Abyad (White Nile)

Lakes

Eastern Equatoria

JUBA

Central Equatoria

Lake Turkana

Gibē Wenz

Genal Wenz

Awara Plain

SOMALIA

MOGADISHU

Woyamdero Plain

KENYA

Wamba

Jubbada

Webi Shabeelle

UGANDA

LAKE ALBERT

Lake Kyoga

Eldoret

Nakuru

Nyeri

Tana

Bilesha Plain

Jubba

Kismaayo

KAMPALA

Kisumu

NAIROBI

Ngangerabeli Plain

Ras Jumbo

Nord Kivu

Lake Edward

LAKE VICTORIA

Rift

Ngorongoro

RWANDA

KIGALI

Speke Gulf

Mwanza

Serengeti Plain

Mt Kilimanjaro

Ras Ngomeni

Lake Kivu

Bukavu

GITEGA

Bujumbura

BURUNDI

Uvira

Arusha

Masai Steppe

Mombasa

LAKE TANGANYIKA

TANZANIA

DODOMA

Morogoro

Tanga

Zanzibar
Zanzibar Island

DAR ES SALAAM

Lukuga

Shuguri Falls

Farquhar Islands

> With the longest coastline on the African mainland, many Somalians are fishermen.

> Women sell coffee beans in a market in Ethiopia, where coffee is the largest crop.

> Mombasa has been an important port for over a thousand years.

DID YOU KNOW? Only around one out of every 17 people in Eritrea owns a mobile phone, the lowest number in any country in the world.

Central Africa

With the equator running through its heart, most of this region has a hot, wet climate. Vast rain forests are fringed by woodland, savanna, and farmland. Many different languages are heard in Central Africa, from Lingala, spoken by 70 million people, to Geme, spoken in just two villages.

Biafra

● Calab

MALABO

Biok

Corisco Islar
Corisco B

LIBREVILL

Mountain Gorillas

Mountain gorillas are among the world's most endangered species, with only about 1,000 animals left in the wild. They live in the Virunga Mountains, a chain of volcanoes that runs through the Democratic Republic of the Congo, Rwanda, and Uganda. The gorillas are threatened by the loss of their forest habitat, hunting, and diseases caught from tourists and farm animals.

Baby gorillas stay with their mother for the first 3 or 4 years.

Congo Rain Forest

The Congo Rain Forest covers a vast region of Central Africa, from the Democratic Republic of the Congo to Cameroon. It is the world's second largest rain forest, after the Amazon.

At 4,700 km (2,920 miles) long, the Congo River is the second longest river in Africa.

Around 10,000 species of tropical plants live in the Congo Rain Forest.

CITY FOCUS: YAOUNDÉ

Status: Capital of Cameroon
Population: 2.8 million
Official languages: English and French
Founded: 1888
Currency: Central African franc
Landmark: Ministry No. 2 Building

Ministry No. 2

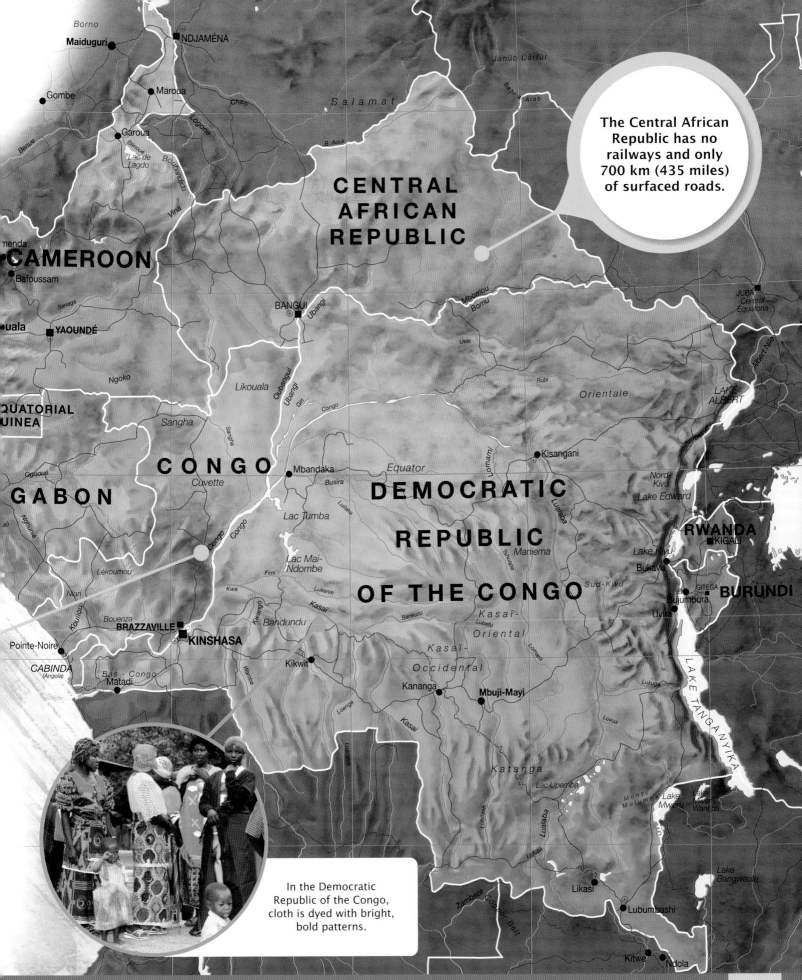

The Central African Republic has no railways and only 700 km (435 miles) of surfaced roads.

In the Democratic Republic of the Congo, cloth is dyed with bright, bold patterns.

DID YOU KNOW? Once ruled by French-speaking Belgium, the Democratic Republic of the Congo is the country outside France with the most French-speakers: 42 million.

27

South-Central Africa

This region's landscape ranges from mountains to plains, covered by desert, grassland, and forest. Some countries here have unusually straight borders. This was brought about when, during the 19th and early 20th centuries, European countries divided Africa between them, often using a ruler and a map.

The Skeleton Coast

The northern coast of Namibia is known as the Skeleton Coast. The wrecks of more than a thousand ships lie on the beach, victims of ocean fogs and rocks. Sea fogs wrap the coast for much of the year, caused by a cold ocean current meeting the hot, damp air blowing from the land. The air is cooled so it can no longer hold all its moisture, which condenses into water droplets.

Namibia is one of the few countries with a capital, Windhoek, almost exactly in the middle of the country.

Local Namibians call the Skeleton Coast "The Land God Made in Anger."

DID YOU KNOW? Lake Nyasa, in Malawi, Mozambique, and Tanzania, has more species of fish than any other lake—over 1,000.

CITY FOCUS: HARARE

Status: Capital of Zimbabwe
Population: 1.6 million
Official languages: 16, including Shona, Ndebele, and English
Founded: 1890
Currency: Zimdollar
Landmark: Heroes' Acre, a monument to those who died fighting for independence from European rule, 1964 to 1979

Central Harare

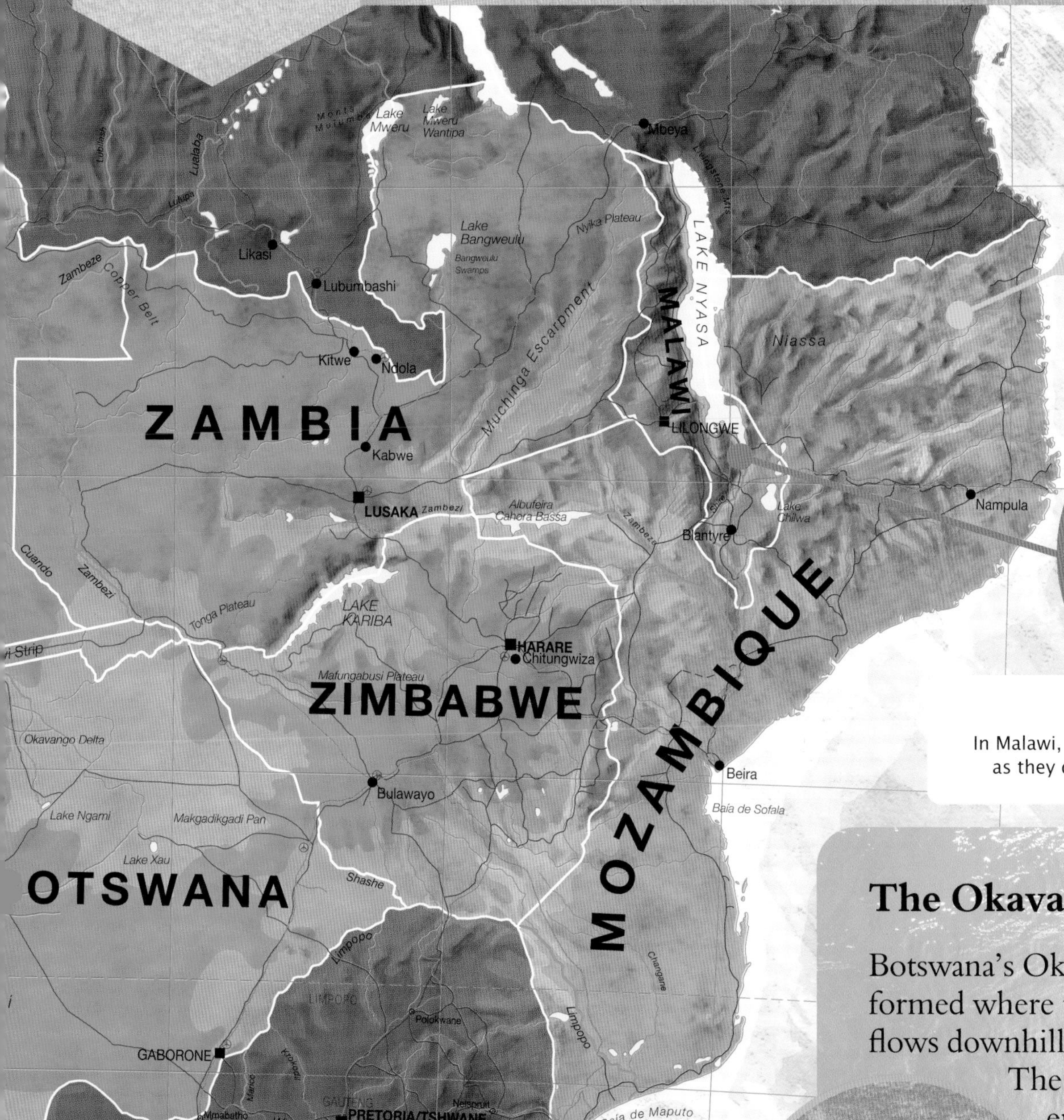

In Mozambique, 80 percent of people work on small, family farms.

In Malawi, Nyau performers wear masks as they dance and kick up the dust.

The Okavango Delta

Botswana's Okavango Delta is formed where the Okavango River flows downhill into a vast trough. The water has no sea to empty into, so it has created a swamp.

Hippos and other water-loving animals live in the delta.

29

South Africa

Much of South Africa is on a vast plateau, at least 1,000 m (3,300 ft) high. It is edged by the steep slopes of the Great Escarpment. South Africa is often called the "rainbow nation" because of its many different peoples and languages. South Africans are employed in industries such as farming, manufacturing, tourism, scientific research, and mining.

Diamonds

Diamond mining is one of South Africa's most important industries. Diamonds are formed from carbon, deep inside the Earth. They can be forced toward the surface by eruptions. In 1871, diamonds were found in the rock near Kimberley. To get them out, 50,000 miners used shovels to dig a hole 240 m (790 ft) into the ground.

The old diamond mine near Kimberley is known as the Big Hole.

Orange

Bushma

NORT

St Helena Bay

Cape Columbine

CAPE TOWN

WEST

Cape of Good Hope

False Bay

Nguni Stick-Fighting

Stick-fighting is a martial art that is traditional to the Nguni people of South Africa. As a boy, Nelson Mandela (1918–2013), the country's first black president, enjoyed the sport.

Performing in traditional clothes, these fighters use sticks both to attack and to defend.

DID YOU KNOW? South Africa is the only country with three capitals: Cape Town (home of parliament), Pretoria (home of the president), and Bloemfontein (home of the highest law court).

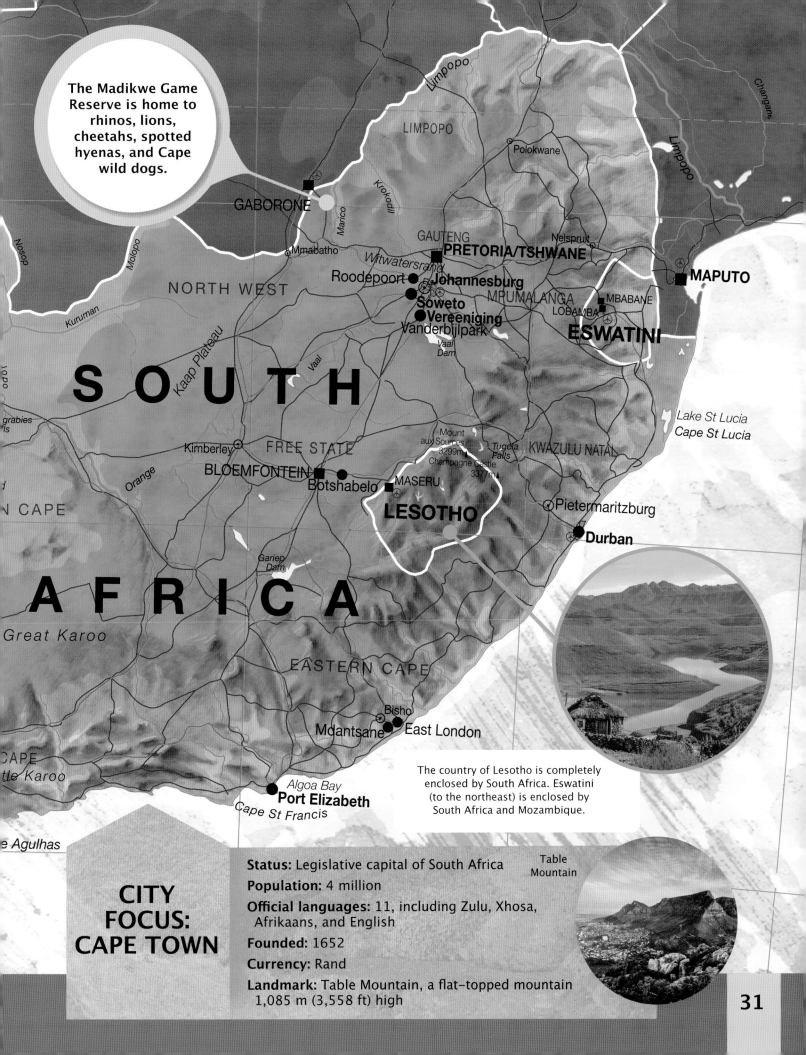

The Madikwe Game Reserve is home to rhinos, lions, cheetahs, spotted hyenas, and Cape wild dogs.

LIMPOPO

Limpopo

Polokwane

GABORONE

Nosop

Molopo

Mmabatho

Marico

Krokodil

GAUTENG

Nelspruit

PRETORIA/TSHWANE

MAPUTO

Witwatersrand

NORTH WEST

Roodepoort

Johannesburg

MPUMALANGA

MBABANE

LOBAMBA

Kuruman

Soweto

Vereeniging

Vanderbijlpark

Vaal Dam

ESWATINI

Kaap Plateau

Vaal

SOUTH

grabies
ls

Kimberley

FREE STATE

Mount aux Sources 3299m

Champagne Castle 3377m

Tugela Falls

KWAZULU NATAL

Lake St Lucia
Cape St Lucia

BLOEMFONTEIN

Botshabelo

MASERU

Orange

Gariep Dam

LESOTHO

Pietermaritzburg

N CAPE

AFRICA

Durban

Great Karoo

EASTERN CAPE

CAPE
tle Karoo

Bisho

Mdantsane

East London

The country of Lesotho is completely enclosed by South Africa. Eswatini (to the northeast) is enclosed by South Africa and Mozambique.

Algoa Bay
Port Elizabeth

Cape St Francis

e Agulhas

Status: Legislative capital of South Africa

Population: 4 million

Table Mountain

CITY FOCUS: CAPE TOWN

Official languages: 11, including Zulu, Xhosa, Afrikaans, and English

Founded: 1652

Currency: Rand

Landmark: Table Mountain, a flat-topped mountain 1,085 m (3,558 ft) high

31

Indian Ocean

Many women and girls in Comoros paint their faces with a paste of tree bark, which keeps off the sun and mosquitoes.

The third largest of the world's oceans, the Indian Ocean is bounded to the west by Africa, to the north by Asia, to the east by Australia, and to the south by the Southern Ocean. With much of its expanse in the tropics, it is the warmest ocean, and the temperature at the surface rarely falls below 22°C (71°F).

Unique Madagascar

The island country of Madagascar lies around 400 km (250 miles) off the east coast of Africa. Until 88 million years ago, Madagascar was joined to India. Since the Earth's formation, the movement of tectonic plates has broken and joined the land masses many times. After splitting from India, around 90 percent of Madagascar's animals and plants evolved, or slowly changed, to be unique.

Like all lemurs, the ring-tailed lemur lives only in Madagascar. Lemurs are distantly related to monkeys and apes.

CITY FOCUS: PORT LOUIS

Port Louis

Status: Capital of Mauritius

Population: 149,000

Official language: None, but Mauritian Creole (a mix of French, African, and Asian languages), French, and English are widely spoken

Founded: 1638

Currency: Mauritian rupee

Landmark: Fort Adelaide, a hilltop fort built by the British army in 1840

Map labels: MEDITERRANEAN S, NIGERIA, CAMEROON, CENTRAL AFRICAN REPUBLIC, Bioko, EQUATORIAL GUINEA, Príncipe, São Tomé, Annobón, GABON, CABINDA, DEMOCRATIC REPUBLIC OF THE CONGO, ANGOLA, ZAM, NAMIBIA, BOTSWANA, LESOTH, SOUTH AFRIC

DID YOU KNOW? There are six independent countries among the islands of the Indian Ocean: Comoros, Madagascar, Mauritius, and Seychelles, in Africa; and Maldives and Sri Lanka in Asia.

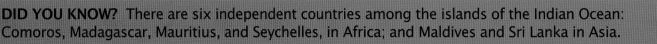

The Maldives are a chain of 26 atolls, spreading over 298 sq km (115 sq miles).

The Indian Ocean has many atolls, including in the island country of Seychelles (pictured).

Coral Atolls

A coral atoll is a ring-shaped coral reef. Plants, animals, and people can live on an atoll. Coral reefs are made from the bony skeletons of tiny animals called coral polyps. Atolls often form around an underwater volcano, which later sinks beneath the water or is worn away.

North America

North America is home to 23 independent countries, from Canada in the north to Panama in the south. This region includes Central America, which is the narrow strip of land (called an isthmus) stretching to South America. The 7,000 islands of the Caribbean Sea are also considered to be part of North America.

The Great Lakes

The five Great Lakes—Superior, Michigan, Huron, Erie, and Ontario—are on the border between the United States and Canada. They are the world's largest group of freshwater lakes, with a total area of 244,100 sq km (94,250 sq miles). The lakes formed around 14,000 years ago as Earth's climate warmed after an ice age. Great sheets of ice had carved hollows into the land. As the ice melted, the hollows filled with water.

Crisp Point Lighthouse was built in 1904 to keep ships safe on stormy Lake Superior, the world's largest freshwater lake.

The Rocky Mountains

The Rocky Mountains stretch for 3,000 km (1,900 miles) from western Canada to the southwestern United States. The mountain range formed 80 million to 55 million years ago as Earth's tectonic plates moved beneath. This movement slowly pushed up mountains, a bit like the way a hand pushing on a tablecloth makes it wrinkle.

Male Rocky Mountain elks can grow antlers up to 1.2 m (4 ft) long.

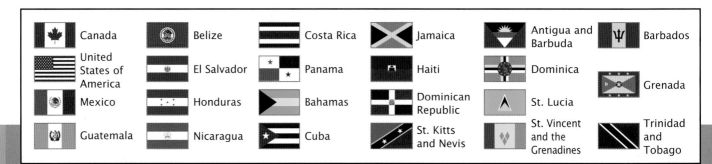

Canada	Belize	Costa Rica	Jamaica	Antigua and Barbuda		Barbados
United States of America	El Salvador	Panama	Haiti	Dominica		
Mexico	Honduras	Bahamas	Dominican Republic	St. Lucia		Grenada
Guatemala	Nicaragua	Cuba	St. Kitts and Nevis	St. Vincent and the Grenadines		Trinidad and Tobago

UNITED STATES
OF AMERICA

C A N A D A

UNITED STATES
OF AMERICA

NORTH ATLANTIC
OCEAN

THE BAHAMAS

MEXICO

CUBA

DOMINICAN REPUBLIC

HAITI

ST KITTS & NEVIS
ANTIGUA & BARBUDA

BELIZE   JAMAICA
HONDURAS

DOMINICA

GUATEMALA

ST LUCIA
BARBADOS

ST VINCENT & THE
GRENADINES

GRENADA

NICARAGUA

EL SALVADOR

COSTA RICA

TRINIDAD & TOBAGO

P A C I F I C

O C E A N

PANAMA

DID YOU KNOW? Possibly around 20,000 years ago, the first people reached North
America by walking from Asia into Alaska, across land that is now underwater.

35

Canada

In the territory of Nunavut, two-thirds of people speak the indigenous language Inuktitut.

With an area of 9.98 million sq km (3.85 million sq miles), Canada is the world's second largest country, after Russia. Most of Canada is covered by forest and tundra, where few people live. More than four out of every five Canadians live in one of the country's cities.

Totem Poles

People were living in Canada for at least 14,000 years before the arrival of the first European settlers, who were mainly from Britain and France. Canada's earliest inhabitants are known as indigenous peoples. Along the west coast, the indigenous peoples have a tradition of carving totem poles from the trunks of Pacific red cedar trees. The poles show family histories and characters from myths.

Many totem poles feature Thunderbird, a powerful creature that can make thunder with its wings.

Parliament Hill

CITY FOCUS: OTTAWA

Status: Capital of Canada
Population: 1.3 million
Official languages: English and French
Founded: 1826
Currency: Canadian dollar
Landmark: Parliament Hill, home to the Parliament of Canada

Ice Hockey

The sport of ice hockey grew out of stick and ball games played in Britain and by indigenous peoples. The first indoor ice hockey match took place in Montréal, Canada, in 1875.

Ice hockey is Canada's most popular winter sport.

Horseshoe Falls, one of the three Niagara Falls, is the most powerful falls in North America.

Cape Thomas Hubbard
Axel Heiberg Island
Ellef Ringnes Island
Amund Ringnes Island
Cape Isachsen
Elizabeth
Bathurst Island
Melville Sound
Stefansson Island
Cornwallis Island
Devon Island
Somerset Island
Prince of Wales Island
Gateshead Island
McClintock Channel
King William Island
Queen Maud Gulf
Kane Basin
Smith Sound
Kap Alexander
Kap Parry
Carey Øer
Cape Sherard
Lancaster Sound
Bylot Island
Cape Dyer

Baffin Island

Spicer Islands
Prince Charles Island
Cape Wilson
Foxe Basin
Nettilling Lake
Angijak Island
Cumberland Sound
Cape Mercy
Temieux Islands
Edgell Island
Iqaluit
Meta Incognita Peninsula
Everett Mountains
Button Islands
Killinik Island
Cape Hopes Advance
Resolution Island
North Aulatsivik Island

NUNAVUT

Foxe Channel
Mill Island
Southampton Island
Seahorse Point
Hudson Strait
Baker Lake
Dubawnt Lake
Yathkyed Lake
Nueltin Lake
Cape Low
Coats Island
Mansel Island
Ungava Bay
Ottawa Islands

Hudson Bay

Péninsula d'Ungava
Ungava Mountains

Reindeer Lake
Southern Indian Lake
Cape Tatnam
Hopewell Islands
Sleeper Islands
King George Islands
North Belcher Islands
Belcher Islands
Nastapoka Islands

CANADA

MANITOBA

Cape Henrietta Maria
Long Island
La Grande
James Bay
Akimiski Island

Lake Winnipeg
Lake Winnipegosis
Nelson
Severn
Albany
Winnipeg
Lake Manitoba
Lake of the Woods

ONTARIO

QUÉBEC

St Lawrence
Laval
Sherbrooke
Montréal
OTTAWA
Québec
Kingston

Thunder Bay
St Ignace Island
Michipicoten Island
Lake Nipigon

NEWFOUNDLAND AND LABRADOR

Lake Melville
Belle Isle
Cape Bauld
Grey Islands
Fogo Island
Newfoundland
St John's
Île d'Anticosti
Cap Gaspé
Îles de la Madeleine
St-Pierre et Miquelon (St. Pierre and Miquelon) (Fr)
St-Pierre
Cape Breton Island
PRINCE EDWARD ISLAND
Prince Edward Island
NEW BRUNSWICK
Moncton
Fredericton
Saint John
NOVA SCOTIA
Halifax
Sable Island (N.S.)
Grand Manan Island
Cape Sable

NORTH DAKOTA
Bismarck
Fargo
MINNESOTA
Minneapolis
St Paul
SOUTH DAKOTA
Pierre
Sioux Falls
IOWA
WISCONSIN
Green Bay
Milwaukee
Madison
Rockford
Chicago
MICHIGAN
LAKE HURON
Strait of Mackinac
Oshawa
Toronto
LAKE ONTARIO
Hamilton
Brampton
London
Detroit
Toledo
Cleveland
LAKE ERIE
Erie
PENNSYLVANIA
Rochester
Syracuse
Albany
NEW YORK
Hartford
RHODE ISLAND
Nantucket Island
New York
Newark
Trenton
Philadelphia
Harrisburg
Montpelier
Concord
Boston
Providence
Bridgeport
MAINE
Gunung of Maine

DID YOU KNOW? A leaf from a maple tree, found in forests across Canada, has been on the national flag since 1965.

United States: Northeast

The United States' many industries and resources have made it the world's wealthiest country. It is divided into 50 states, each with its own government, which shares power with the national government, in Washington, DC. This city is independent from all the states and is in its own district: District of Columbia (DC).

One World Trade Center

The tallest building in North America is One World Trade Center, in the United States' biggest city, New York. This skyscraper stands on the site of the Twin Towers of the original World Trade Center, which collapsed after a terrorist attack. The new building contains offices, shops, and restaurants.

One World Trade Center is 1,776 ft (541 m) tall. Its height in feet refers to the date that the United States signed its Declaration of Independence from Great Britain: 1776.

Oshawa
Toronto
Oakville
Hamilton
Niagara Fal
Buffalo
Erie
PENNS
Pittsburgh

CITY FOCUS: WASHINGTON, DC

Status: Capital of the United States
Population: 711,000
Official language: None
Founded: 1790
Currency: United States dollar
Landmark: The Capitol Building, where lawmakers meet in the United States Congress

Capitol Building

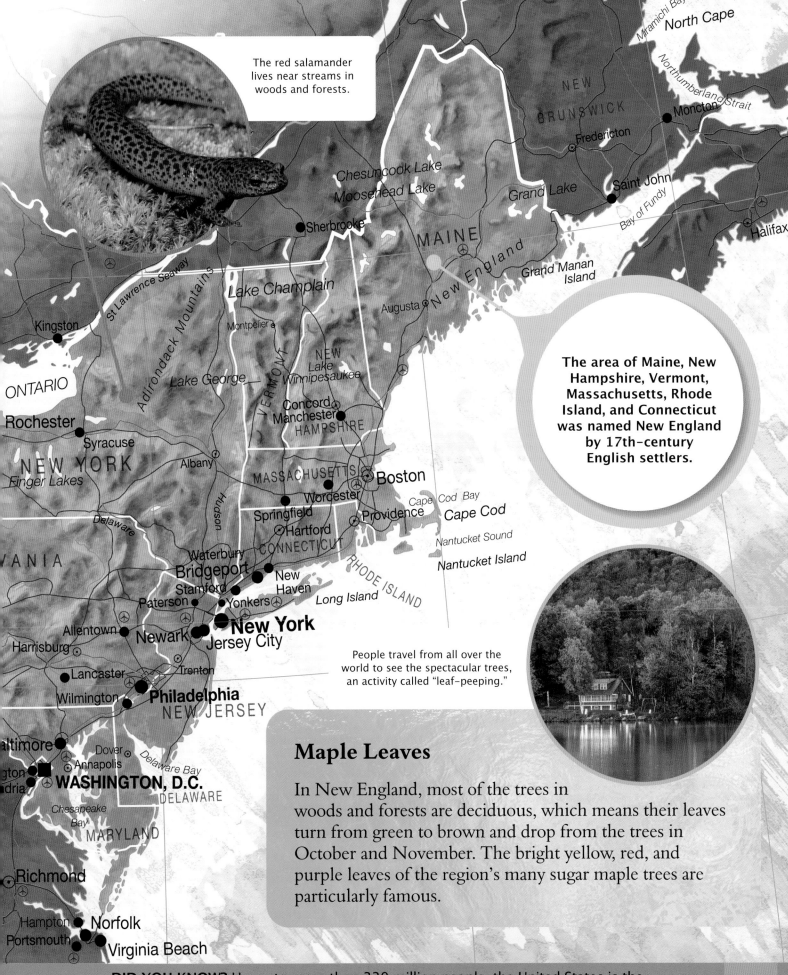

The red salamander lives near streams in woods and forests.

North Cape

Miramichi Bay

NEW BRUNSWICK

Northumberland Strait

Moncton

Fredericton

Chesuncook Lake

Moosehead Lake

Grand Lake

Saint John

Bay of Fundy

Halifax

MAINE

New England

Sherbrooke

Grand Manan Island

St Lawrence Seaway

Lake Champlain

Augusta

The area of Maine, New Hampshire, Vermont, Massachusetts, Rhode Island, and Connecticut was named New England by 17th-century English settlers.

Kingston

Montpelier

VERMONT

NEW Lake Winnipesaukee

ONTARIO

Lake George

Adirondack Mountains

Concord

Manchester

HAMPSHIRE

Rochester

Syracuse

Albany

NEW YORK

Finger Lakes

MASSACHUSETTS

Boston

Worcester

Cape Cod Bay

Springfield

Providence

Cape Cod

Hudson

Hartford

Nantucket Sound

Delaware

CONNECTICUT

Nantucket Island

Waterbury

RHODE ISLAND

Bridgeport

Stamford

New Haven

Long Island

VANIA

Paterson

Yonkers

Allentown

Newark

New York

Harrisburg

Jersey City

People travel from all over the world to see the spectacular trees, an activity called "leaf-peeping."

Lancaster

Trenton

Wilmington

Philadelphia

NEW JERSEY

ltimore

Dover

Delaware Bay

gton

Annapolis

WASHINGTON, D.C.

dria

DELAWARE

Chesapeake Bay

Maple Leaves

MARYLAND

In New England, most of the trees in woods and forests are deciduous, which means their leaves turn from green to brown and drop from the trees in October and November. The bright yellow, red, and purple leaves of the region's many sugar maple trees are particularly famous.

Richmond

Hampton

Norfolk

Portsmouth

Virginia Beach

DID YOU KNOW? Home to more than 330 million people, the United States is the country with the third largest population, after China and India.

39

United States: South

Most of the southern United States has hot, humid summers and short winters. The forested Appalachian Mountains run down the east side of this region. The low, flat land along the southern coast is crisscrossed by bayous, or slow-moving streams and marshes.

Mardi Gras

Every year just before Lent, the city of New Orleans, in Louisiana, celebrates Mardi Gras (French for "Fat Tuesday"). Lent is a time when Christians traditionally give up luxuries. During the party, people parade through the streets in fantastical costumes, while playing music and dancing.

Mardi Gras was first celebrated by early French settlers, but the costumes have been shaped by African American and Native American traditions.

CITY FOCUS: MIAMI

Status: City in the state of Florida

Population: 5.5 million

Official language: English

Founded: 1825

Currency: United States dollar

Landmark: Eye-catching geometric buildings in South Beach, built in the 1930s in Art Deco style

South Beach

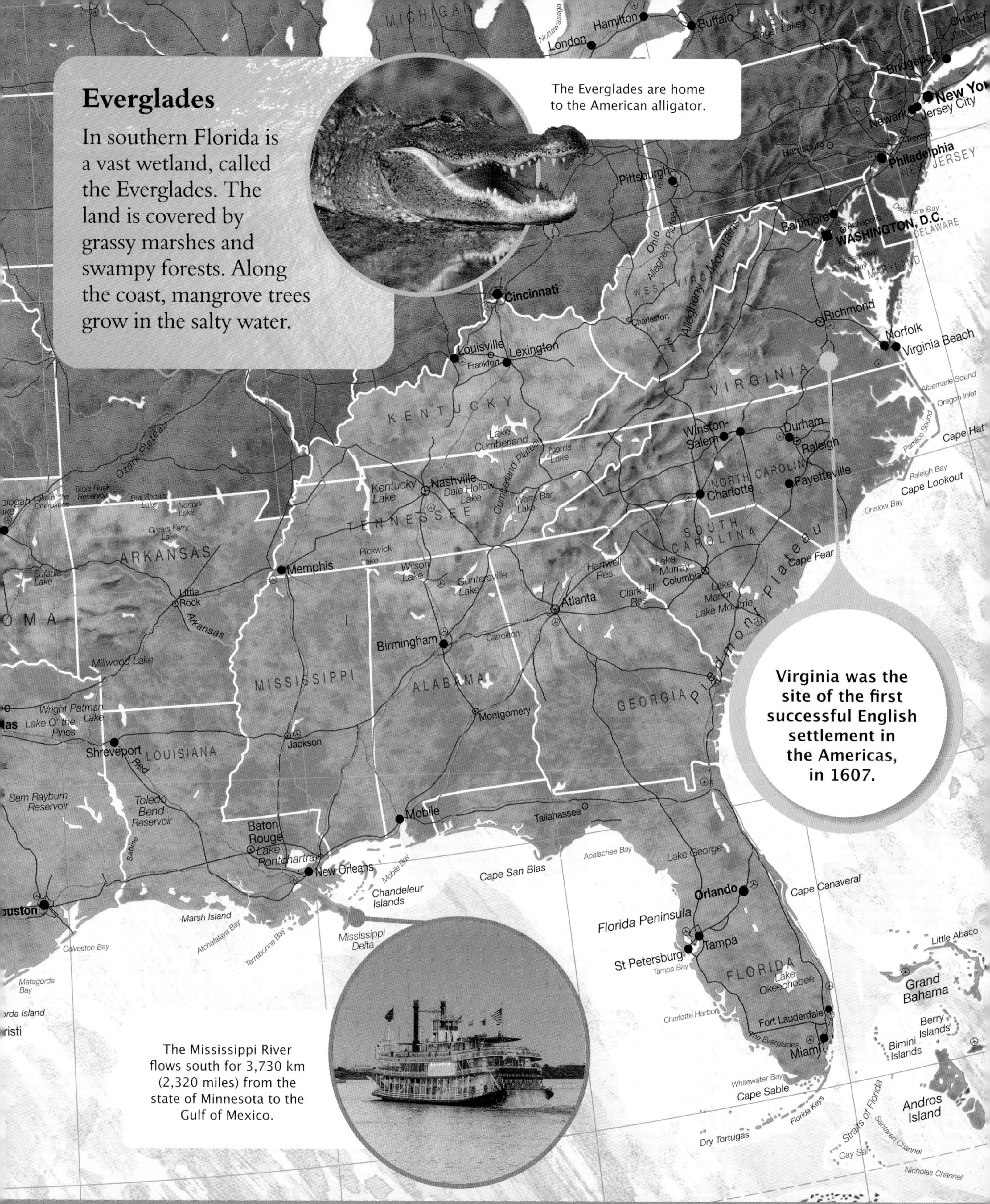

Everglades

In southern Florida is a vast wetland, called the Everglades. The land is covered by grassy marshes and swampy forests. Along the coast, mangrove trees grow in the salty water.

The Everglades are home to the American alligator.

Virginia was the site of the first successful English settlement in the Americas, in 1607.

The Mississippi River flows south for 3,730 km (2,320 miles) from the state of Minnesota to the Gulf of Mexico.

DID YOU KNOW? The southern United States was the birthplace of blues music, which grew from the work songs of African American slaves in the 19th century.

United States: Midwest

The word "Dakota" comes from the Dakota (meaning "friends") Native American people.

The midwestern states lie in the largely flat region, known as a plain, between the Appalachian Mountains in the east and the Rocky Mountains in the west. Much of the land is covered by large farms, but midwestern cities are focussed on manufacturing, including products such as cars and machinery.

Tornado Alley

This region is often called "Tornado Alley" because of its many tornadoes. Tornadoes form in the swirling air below thunderclouds. The Midwest is where warm, humid air from the south meets cool, dry air from Canada and the Rocky Mountains. As the warm air cools, its moisture turns to liquid— or condenses—into thunderclouds.

From left to right, the sculpture shows George Washington, Thomas Jefferson, Theodore Roosevelt, and Abraham Lincoln.

A tornado forms when hot air rises quickly below a thundercloud, creating a spinning funnel.

Mount Rushmore

From 1927 to 1941, sculptor Gutzon Borglum and 400 helpers carved the faces of four presidents of the United States into Mount Rushmore, in South Dakota. The heads are 18 m (60 ft) high.

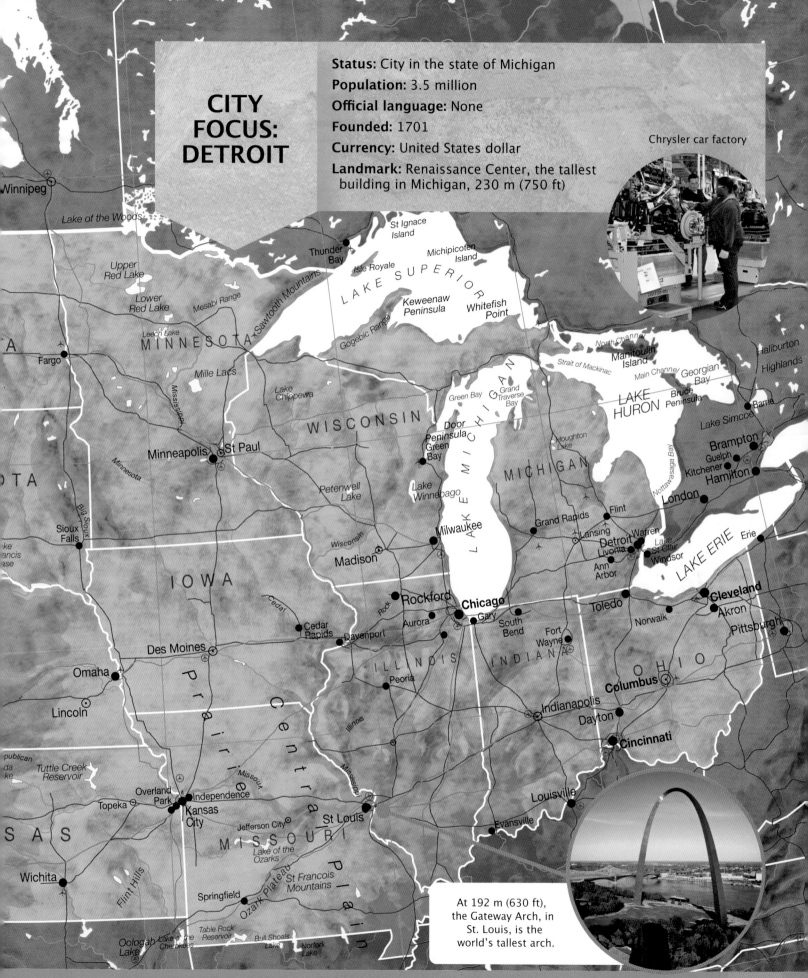

CITY FOCUS: DETROIT

Status: City in the state of Michigan

Population: 3.5 million

Official language: None

Founded: 1701

Currency: United States dollar

Landmark: Renaissance Center, the tallest building in Michigan, 230 m (750 ft)

Chrysler car factory

At 192 m (630 ft), the Gateway Arch, in St. Louis, is the world's tallest arch.

DID YOU KNOW? The world's first skyscraper was the Home Insurance Building, built in 1885 in Chicago, which reached 55 m (180 ft) tall.

United States: West

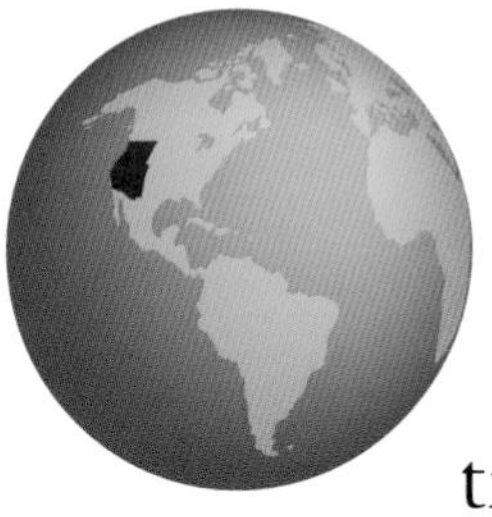

This region lies between the Pacific Ocean coast and the Rocky Mountains. In the northwest are temperate rain forests, where heavy rain enables trees, shrubs, mosses, and ferns to grow thickly. In contrast, the hot, dry southwest is where the Mojave and Sonoran Deserts lie.

The Grand Canyon

The Grand Canyon, in Arizona, was worn away by the Colorado River over about 4 million years. The fast-flowing water, as well as the pebbles and rocks it carried, cut a deeper and deeper canyon. Today, the canyon is up to 1,857 m (6,093 ft) deep, up to 29 km (18 miles) wide, and 446 km (277 miles) long.

Around 5 million people travel to see the Grand Canyon every year.

CITY FOCUS: SAN FRANCISCO

Status: City in the state of California

Population: 4.6 million

Official language: English

Founded: 1776

Currency: United States dollar

Landmark: Golden Gate Bridge, completed in 1937

Golden Gate Bridge

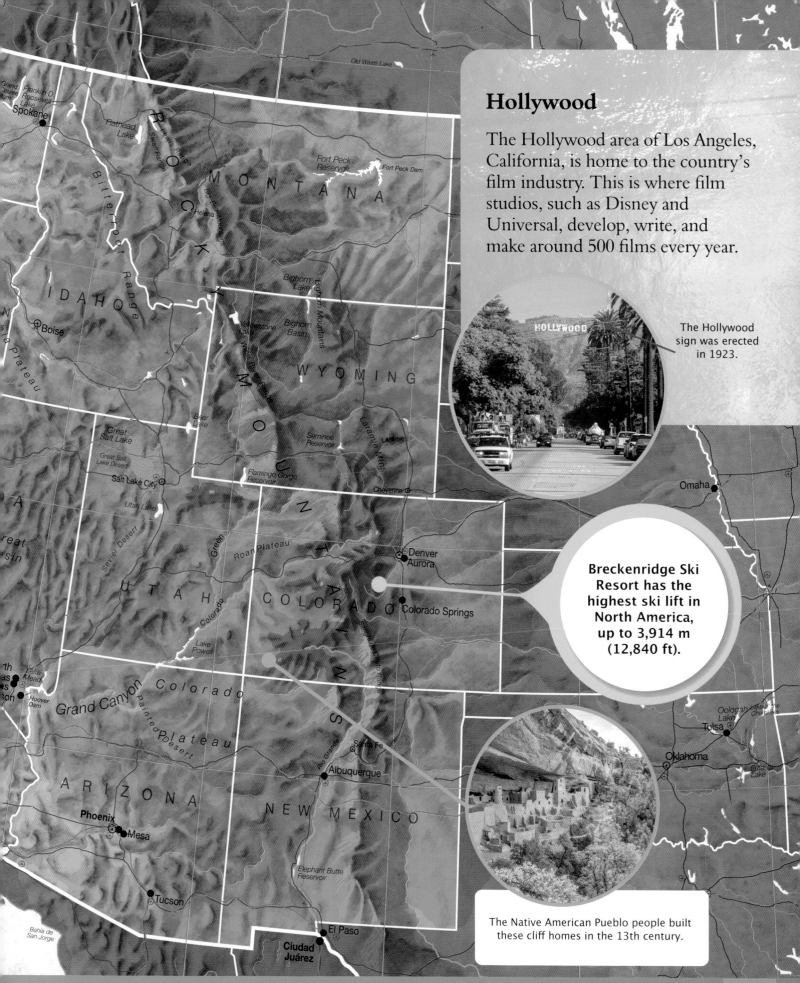

Hollywood

The Hollywood area of Los Angeles, California, is home to the country's film industry. This is where film studios, such as Disney and Universal, develop, write, and make around 500 films every year.

The Hollywood sign was erected in 1923.

Breckenridge Ski Resort has the highest ski lift in North America, up to 3,914 m (12,840 ft).

The Native American Pueblo people built these cliff homes in the 13th century.

DID YOU KNOW? Death Valley, in the Mojave Desert, is one of the world's hottest places, reaching a temperature of 56.7°C (134°F).

45

United States: Alaska

Alaska was home to Inupiat, Yupik, Aleut, and other Alaska Natives when the first Russians settled in the 18th century. In 1867, Russia sold Alaska to the United States. While Alaska's interior is cloaked in coniferous forest, the north and west are covered by tundra.

At 6,190 m (20,310 ft), Denali is the highest mountain in North America.

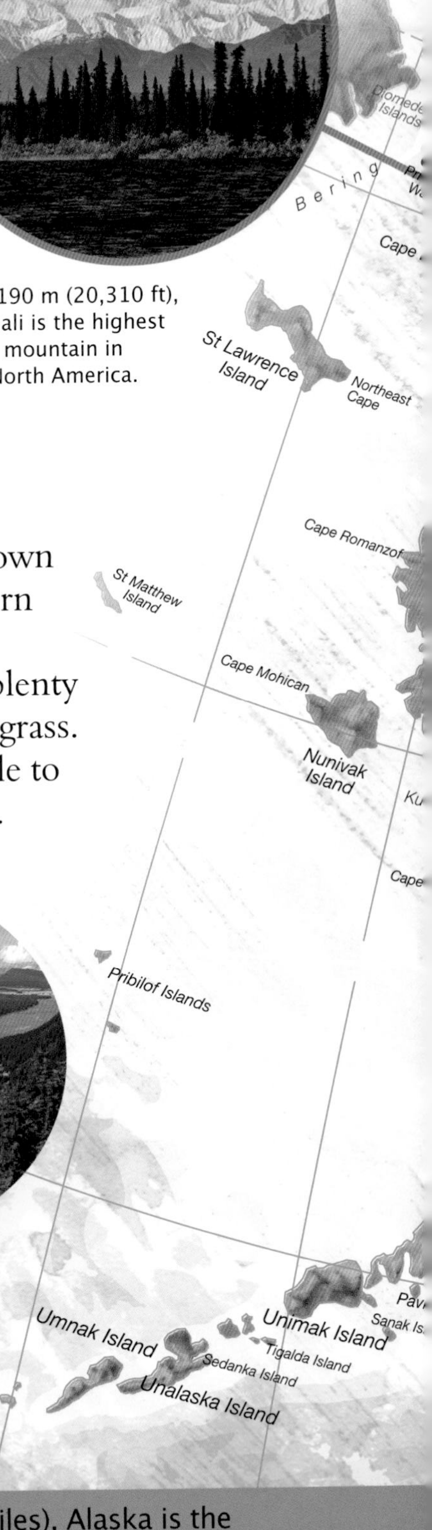

Grizzlies

Grizzly bears, also called North American brown bears, live in Alaska, Canada, and the northern Rocky Mountains. They are most common along the coasts of Alaska, where there are plenty of fish to catch, as well as berries and sedge grass. This is also where the bears grow largest, able to stand up to 3 m (9.8 ft) tall on their hind legs.

At Brooks Falls, in Katmai National Park, grizzlies wait for salmon to leap over the waterfall as they swim up to the lake where they lay eggs.

CITY FOCUS: JUNEAU

Status: Capital of the state of Alaska

Population: 24,000

Official languages: 21, including English, Inupiat, Yupik, and Aleut

Founded: 1881

Currency: United States dollar

Landmark: Mount Juneau, 1,090 m (3,576 ft) tall

Juneau

Map labels: Diomede Islands, Bering, Cape, St Lawrence Island, Northeast Cape, Cape Romanzof, St Matthew Island, Cape Mohican, Nunivak Island, Ku, Cape, Pribilof Islands, Umnak Island, Tigalda Island, Sedanka Island, Unalaska Island, Unimak Island, Sanak Is., Pav

DID YOU KNOW? With an area of 1,717,856 sq km (663,268 sq miles), Alaska is the largest state in the United States, but the least densely populated.

Oil and Gas

Alaska makes most of its money from oil and natural gas, which are drilled and pumped from the ground and seabed in northern Alaska and the Cook Inlet in the south. These fossil fuels formed over millions of years from dead plants that were buried under layers of mud. Oil and gas can be burned to make heat.

Oil is pumped from northern Alaska to the port of Valdez, in southern Alaska, along the 1,288-km (800-mile) Trans-Alaska Pipeline.

There are 57 volcanoes on the Aleutian Islands, which stretch across the Pacific Ocean to Russia.

Mexico

Mexico was home to one of the world's early civilizations. From 1500 to 400 BCE, the Olmecs lived in cities, constructed grand buildings, and made beautiful art. Later, the Maya and Aztecs controlled the region, until they were conquered by the Spanish in the 16th century.

The Maya

From around 750 BCE, the Maya were building great cities in southeastern Mexico and northern Central America. They built pyramid-shaped temples to the gods, observatories for watching the stars, and courts for playing ball games. They also developed their own writing, mathematics, and a calendar with 365 days, based on their studies of the Sun.

Built between the 8th and 12th centuries CE, this pyramid in the Maya city of Chichén Itzá was dedicated to the serpent god Kukulkan.

CITY FOCUS: MEXICO CITY

Status: Capital of Mexico

Population: 21 million

Official languages: Spanish, plus 63 indigenous languages

Founded: 1325

Currency: Mexican peso

Landmark: Metropolitan Cathedral, built from 1573 to 1813

Mexico City and Popocatépetl volcano

48

During the festival, people paint their faces like skulls, to remember that death is a natural part of life.

Day of the Dead

At the start of November, Mexicans celebrate Día de Muertos ("Day of the Dead"), when the spirits of dead loved ones are believed to wake and join the festivities. People tell stories about dead friends and family, and take gifts of food and flowers to their graves.

Southern Mexico was the first place where maize, also called corn, was planted, in around 8000 BCE.

Corpus Christí

Nuevo Laredo

Monclova
Presa Falcon

Monterrey
Guadalupe
Reynosa

Torreón
Saltillo

Bolsón de Mapimí

Durango

Llanos de Tamaulipas

Zacatecas
Ciudad Victoria

M E X I C O

Aguascalientes
San Luis Potosí

Tampico
Cárdenas

Cape Rojo

León
Irapuato

Guadalajara
Celaya
Querétaro
Pachuca

Laguna de Chapala

Morelia
MEXICO CITY
Ecatépec
Xalapa

Colima
Uruapan
Toluca
Tlaxcala
Puebla
Orizaba
Veracruz

Cuernavaca

Coatzacoalcos

Chilpancingo
Villahermosa

Oaxaca
Istmo de Tehuantepec
Tuxtla Gutiérrez

Acapulco

Golfo de Tehuantepec

Arrecífes Triángulos

Cayos Arcas

Campeche

Bahía de Campeche

Mérida
Cancún

Yucatán Peninsula

Chetumal

Llanos de Tabasco y Campeche

BELIZE
Turneffe Islands

GUATEMALA

Golfo de Honduras

San Pedro Sula

GUATEMALA

Tapachula

SAN SALVADOR
EL SALVADOR

The axolotl is an endangered amphibian, found only in Lake Xochimilco.

DID YOU KNOW? There are more Spanish speakers in Mexico, 130 million, than there are in Spain itself, where there are 47 million.

49

Central America

Seven countries are in Central America: Belize, Guatemala, Honduras, El Salvador, Nicaragua, Costa Rica, and Panama. This tropical region is home to more than 500,000 species of animals and plants. Central America lies along the edges of tectonic plates, resulting in many volcanoes and earthquakes.

Arrecife
Triángu
Bahía de Campeche
del C
Coatzacoalcos
Villahermosa
Tuxtla Gutiérrez
Golfo de Tehuantepec
Tapachula

Panama Canal

Between 1881 and 1914, a canal was dug across Panama to let ships travel quickly between the Atlantic and Pacific Oceans. Work on the 82-km (51-mile) canal was begun by France but finished by the United States. More than 30,000 workers died from disease and accidents during the canal's construction.

When entering the canal, ships pass through gates, called locks, where the water level rises, lifting them from sea level to the higher level of the canal.

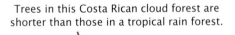

Trees in this Costa Rican cloud forest are shorter than those in a tropical rain forest.

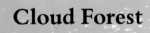

Cloud Forest

Cloud forests are found on mountains in Central America and other tropical regions. Warm air carrying lots of moisture is pushed upward by the mountains. As the air rises, it cools, making the moisture condense into cloud, which wraps the cloud forest in permanent mist.

DID YOU KNOW? Nowhere on the isthmus of Central America is farther than 200 km (125 miles) from the ocean.

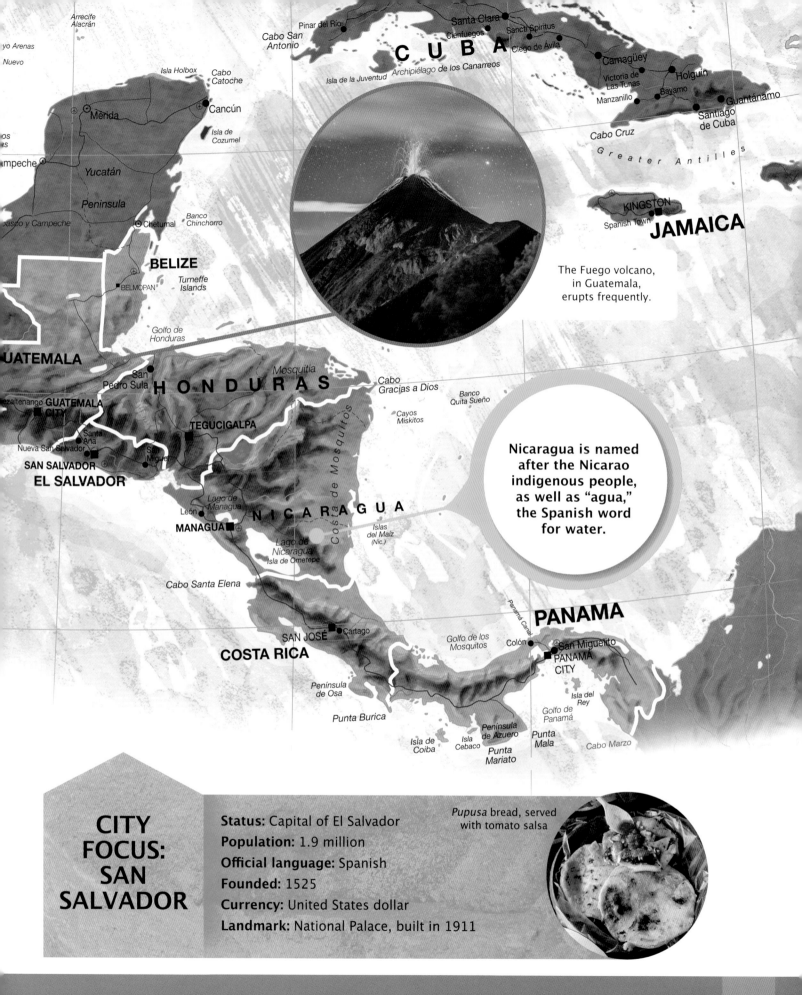

CUBA

Arrecife Alacrán

yo Arenas

Nuevo

Pinar del Río

Cabo San Antonio

Santa Clara

Cienfuegos Sancti Spíritus

Isla de la Juventud Ciego de Ávila

Archipiélago de los Canarreos Camagüey

Victoria de Las Tunas Holguín

Manzanillo Bayamo Guantánamo

Santiago de Cuba

Cabo Cruz

Greater Antilles

Isla Holbox Cabo Catoche

Mérida Cancún

Isla de Cozumel

Yucatán

Peninsula

Chetumal Banco Chinchorro

BELIZE

BELMOPAN Turneffe Islands

Golfo de Honduras

KINGSTON

Spanish Town JAMAICA

The Fuego volcano, in Guatemala, erupts frequently.

GUATEMALA

San Pedro Sula HONDURAS Mosquitia

Cabo Gracias a Dios

Banco Quita Sueño

ezaltenango GUATEMALA CITY TEGUCIGALPA

Cayos Miskitos

Santa Ana

Nueva San Salvador San Miguel

SAN SALVADOR

EL SALVADOR

León Lago de Managua

MANAGUA NICARAGUA

Costa de Mosquitos

Islas del Maíz (Nic.)

Nicaragua is named after the Nicarao indigenous people, as well as "agua," the Spanish word for water.

Lago de Nicaragua Isla de Ometepe

Cabo Santa Elena

Panamá Canal PANAMA

SAN JOSÉ Cartago

Golfo de los Mosquitos

Colón San Miguelito

PANAMA CITY

COSTA RICA

Península de Osa

Punta Burica

Isla del Rey

Golfo de Panamá

Punta Mala Cabo Marzo

Isla de Coiba Isla Cebaco Península de Azuero Punta Mariato

Punta Mala

CITY FOCUS: SAN SALVADOR

Status: Capital of El Salvador

Population: 1.9 million

Official language: Spanish

Founded: 1525

Currency: United States dollar

Landmark: National Palace, built in 1911

Pupusa bread, served with tomato salsa

The Caribbean

There are 13 independent countries in the Caribbean Sea, as well as islands governed by countries such as the United Kingdom, the Netherlands, and France. Important industries in the Caribbean are tourism, banking, and farming. Many Caribbean islanders have African roots.

Volcanic Islands

The Lesser Antilles are a curving chain of islands in the southeastern Caribbean. The islands formed where one tectonic plate pushed under another. The pressure and heat caused melted rock, called magma, to rise to the surface, where it erupted from volcanoes. As the rock cooled and hardened, the volcanoes grew, rising above the sea surface as islands.

The two Piton mountains, on St. Lucia, are made of magma that hardened inside the neck of a volcano.

Spice Island

The small island of Grenada is known as "Spice Island" because it produces 20 percent of the world's nutmeg and mace. Nutmeg is a spice made from the seed of the nutmeg tree, while mace comes from the seed covering.

The first nutmeg trees were brought to Grenada from Indonesia in 1843.

Map labels: NASSA, Andros, HAVANA, Matanzas, Santa Clara, Pinar del Río, Cienfuegos, Camagüe, CUBA, Baya, Sant, Cayman Is. (U.K.), Greate, KINGSTO, JAMAICA, Barra, Carta, Colón, Panama Canal, PANAMA CITY

DID YOU KNOW? The Caribbean is named after the Caribs, a South American people who were living in the Lesser Antilles when Europeans first arrived.

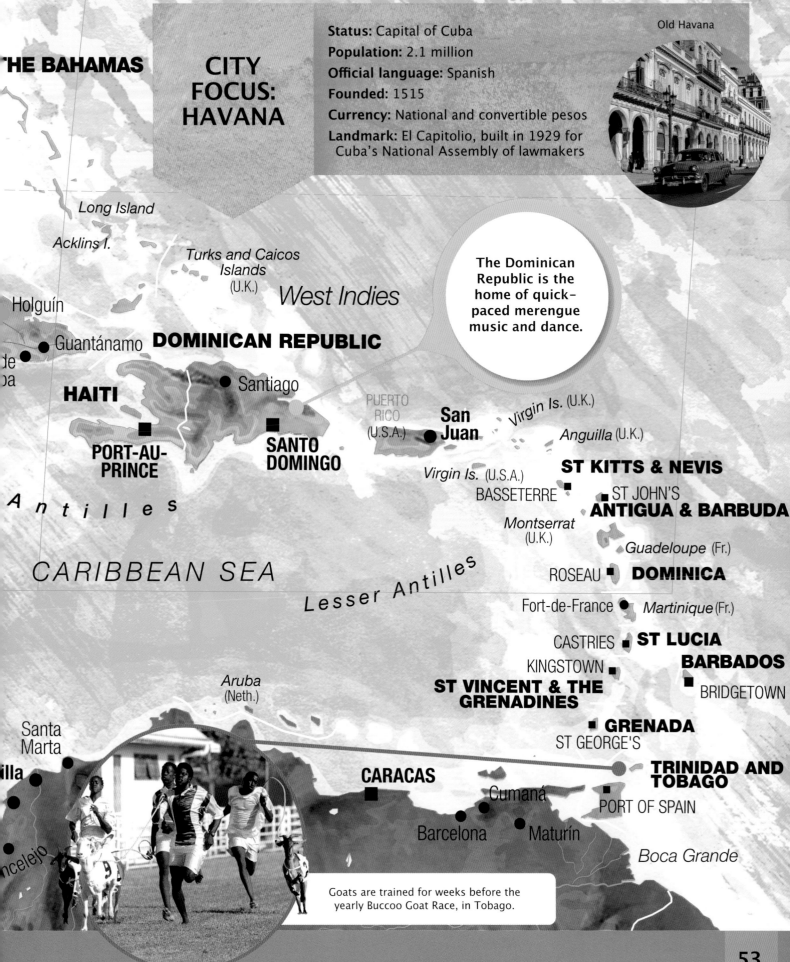

THE BAHAMAS

CITY FOCUS: HAVANA

Old Havana

Status: Capital of Cuba
Population: 2.1 million
Official language: Spanish
Founded: 1515
Currency: National and convertible pesos
Landmark: El Capitolio, built in 1929 for Cuba's National Assembly of lawmakers

Long Island

Acklins I.

Turks and Caicos Islands (U.K.)

West Indies

Holguín

Guantánamo

DOMINICAN REPUBLIC

The Dominican Republic is the home of quick-paced merengue music and dance.

Santiago

HAITI

PUERTO RICO (U.S.A.)

San Juan

Virgin Is. (U.K.)

PORT-AU-PRINCE

SANTO DOMINGO

Anguilla (U.K.)

A n t i l l e s

Virgin Is. (U.S.A.)

ST KITTS & NEVIS

BASSETERRE

ST JOHN'S

ANTIGUA & BARBUDA

Montserrat (U.K.)

Guadeloupe (Fr.)

CARIBBEAN SEA

Lesser Antilles

ROSEAU

DOMINICA

Fort-de-France

Martinique (Fr.)

CASTRIES

ST LUCIA

KINGSTOWN

BARBADOS

Aruba (Neth.)

ST VINCENT & THE GRENADINES

BRIDGETOWN

Santa Marta

GRENADA

ST GEORGE'S

illa

TRINIDAD AND TOBAGO

CARACAS

Cumaná

ncelejo

PORT OF SPAIN

Barcelona

Maturín

Boca Grande

Goats are trained for weeks before the yearly Buccoo Goat Race, in Tobago.

South America

South America reaches from the tropical beaches of Colombia to the icy tundra of southern Chile. The majority of the region's 429 million inhabitants live near the coasts rather than in the rain forest and desert of the interior. Most South Americans are descendants of Spanish and Portuguese settlers, African enslaved workers, and indigenous peoples.

The Andes Mountains

Stretching for 7,000 km (4,300 miles) along the western edge of South America, the Andes are the world's longest mountain range on land. The mountains were formed as two tectonic plates slid under the South American plate, pushing up rock as well as making a chain of volcanoes.

The Andes had formed by about 45 million years ago.

The Amazon River

The Amazon River is home to 2,200 species of fish.

The world's longest river flows around 6,990 km (4,345 miles) from the mountains of Peru to the Atlantic Ocean in Brazil. The river has over 1,100 streams and rivers flowing into it, called tributaries. Every year in the rainy season, the rivers flood the surrounding forest, creating a rich, watery habitat called *várzea*.

	Venezuela		Brazil
	Guyana		Bolivia
	Suriname		Paraguay
	Colombia		Uruguay
	Ecuador		Chile
	Peru		Argentina

DID YOU KNOW? Around nine out of ten South Americans are Christians, a religion brought to the continent by Europeans from the late 15th century.

VENEZUELA

GUYANA

SURINAME

COLOMBIA

ECUADOR

BRAZIL

PERU

BOLIVIA

PACIFIC

OCEAN

PARAGUAY

SOUTH ATLANTIC
OCEAN

URUGUAY

ARGENTINA

CHILE

Venezuela and the Guianas

On South America's north coast is the country of Venezuela, home to rain forest, grasslands, and many industrial cities. To its east is the Guianas region, covering the countries Guyana and Suriname, as well as French Guiana, which is not an independent country but a part of France.

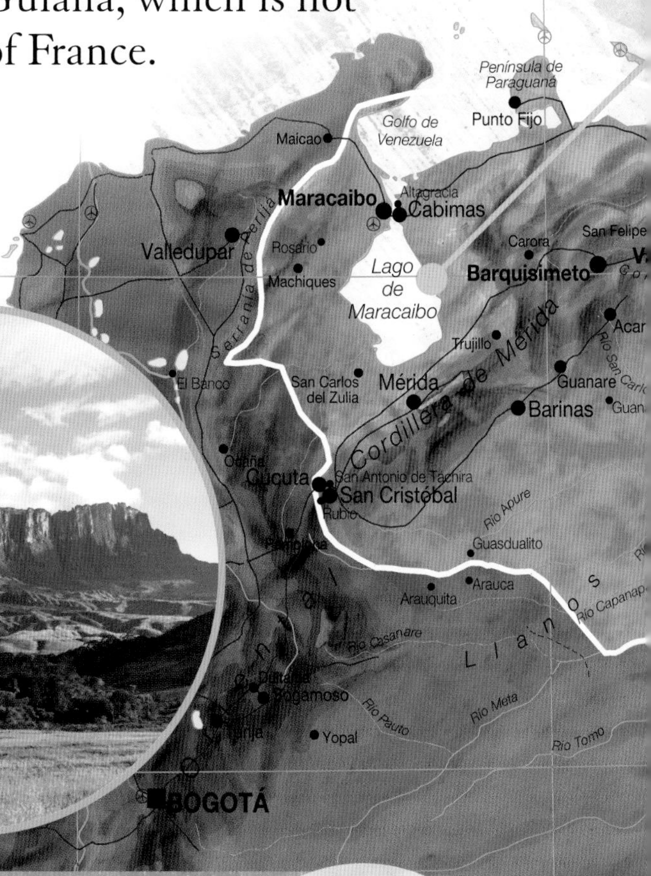

Tepuis

In Venezuela and Guyana are more than 100 flat-topped mountains known as tepuis. Tepui means "house of the gods" in the local Pemon language. Tepuis are the remains of a vast slab of sandstone rock, which has slowly worn away. Over millions of years, the species of animals and plants living on the tepuis were cut off from the rest of the world. Today, many of these species exist nowhere else.

Ayangaik Tepui, in Guyana, is 1,019 m (3,344 ft) high.

CITY FOCUS: CARACAS

Country: Capital of Venezuela

Population: 2.9 million

Official language: Spanish

Founded: 1567

Currency: Venezuelan bolívar

Landmark: Parque Central Complex, the second highest building in South America, 225 m (738 ft) tall

Caracas

Map labels: Península de Paraguaná, Golfo de Venezuela, Punto Fijo, Maicao, Maracaibo, Altagracia, Cabimas, Valledupar, Rosario, Machiques, Lago de Maracaibo, Carora, San Felipe, Barquisimeto, Trujillo, Acar, El Banco, San Carlos del Zulia, Mérida, Guanare, Barinas, Guan, Cordillera de Mérida, Serranía de Perijá, Río San Carlo, Ocaña, Cúcuta, San Antonio de Táchira, San Cristóbal, Rubio, Guasdualito, Arauca, Arauquita, Llanos, Río Apure, Río Casanare, Río Meta, Río Capanap, Río Pauto, Río Tomo, Sogamoso, Yopal, BOGOTÁ, Río Guainía, Mitú

DID YOU KNOW? Guyana is the only South American country where English is the official language, although most people speak Guyana Creole, a mix of English, Dutch, and local languages.

Angel Falls

With a height of 979 m (3,212 ft), Venezuela's Angel Falls is the world's tallest waterfall. The falls' English name comes from the American pilot James Angel, who crash-landed nearby in 1937. It took Angel 11 days to walk to the nearest village.

Angel Falls plunges off the edge of Auyán Tepui.

Huge stores of oil are found deep beneath Lake Maracaibo. Venezuela exports this valuable fuel across the world.

Found only on the tepuis of western Guyana, Beebe's golden rocket frog lives in the leaves of the giant bromeliad.

Suriname is South America's smallest country. More than half its 550,000 inhabitants live in the capital, Paramaribo.

Around four-fifths of Guyana is covered by forest.

Map labels

Islas Los Roques
Isla Blanquilla
GRENADA ST GEORGE'S
Islas Las Aves
Isla Orchila
Isla de Margarita
Islas Los Testigos
Tobago
Isla La Tortuga
La Asunción
Península de Paria
PORT OF SPAIN
Galera Point
Maiquetía
Porlamar
Guíria
Arima
Trinidad
ARACAS Petare
Cumaná
Carúpano
Caripito
San Fernando
Maracay
Los Teques
Barcelona
Puerto La Cruz
Boca de la Serpiente
Maracay
Ocumare del Tuy
Altagracia de Orituco
Aragua de Barcelona
Punta de Mata
Maturín
Delta del Orinoco
San Juan de los Morros
Anaco Cantaura
San Josédé
Tucupita
Valle de la Pascua
Zaraza
El Tigre
Guanipa
El Temblador
Boca Grande
Calabozo
Embalse del Guárico
Pariaguan
Soledad Río Orinoco
Ciudad Guayana
mendi
Upata
Puerto Miranda
San Fernando de Apure
Ciudad Bolívar
Puerto Carreño
Rio Orinoco
GEORGETOWN
Cuyuni
V E N E Z U E L A
Embalse de Guri
Angel Falls (Salto Angel) 979m
G U Y A N A
New Amsterdam
PARAMARIBO
Nieuw Amsterdam
Bartica
Linden
Corriverton
Nieuw Nickerie
Lelydorp
St-Laurent-du-Maroni
Kourou
Puerto Ayacucho
Rio Caroni
Kaieteur Falls
Affobakka
Professor van Blommestein Meer
Cayenne
Matoury
Río Ventuari
Salto Cuquenán
Sierra Maigualida
Essequibo
Corantijn
SURINAME
French Guiana (France)
Rio Negro
Río Orinoco
Canal Casiquiare
Rio Siapa
Frederik Willem IV Vallen
Eilerts de Haan Gebergte
Oranje Gebergte
H I G H L A N D S
Serra Parima
Rio Uaupes
Rio Uaricuera
Serra Acarai
Rio Paru de Oeste
Rio Mapuera
Rio Jari
Serra Tumucumaque
Serra Lombarda
Gran

57

Colombia

The Andes Mountains tower over western Colombia, while to the northeast is the Llanos, a plain covered by tropical grassland. Part of the vast Amazon Rain Forest lies in the southeast. Colombia is one of the wealthiest South American countries, with its people working in industries from banking to shipbuilding.

Biodiversity

Biodiversity is the number of animal and plants species found in a region. Colombia is the second most biodiverse country in the world, after Brazil, which has an area seven times Colombia's. Biodiversity is highest in tropical regions where warmth and rain enable plants and animals to thrive. Colombia's coasts, mountains, and plains also offer a wide range of habitats. With more than 1,850 species of birds, Colombia is home to more bird species than any other country.

The Santa Marta sabrewing hummingbird lives only in Colombia.

Carved between 5 and 400 CE, the 300 statues of gods and animals at St Agustín were placed by graves.

Galeras, close to the city of Pasto, is the most active and dangerous volcano in Colombia.

Map labels

Cabo de la A
Barranquill
Sabanalarga
Cartagena
Turbaco
Arjona
Golfo de Morrosquillo
Sincelejo
Corozal
Golfo del Darién
Lorica
Cereté
Sahagún
Montería
Turbo
Río Sinú
Río San Jorge
Río Cauca
Barranc
Cabo Marzo
Río Atrato
Bello
Medellín
Envigado
Quibdó
Manizales
Cartago
Pereira
Armenia
Fusaga
Ibagué
Gi
Esp
Buga
Tuluá
Buenaventura
Yumbo
Cali
Palmira
C
Isla Gorgona
Neiva
Punta Guascama
Popayán
Tumaco
Río Patía
Cabo Manglares
Florencia
Mocoa
Esmeraldas
Ipiales
Cabo de San Francisco
Río Esmeraldas
Tulcán
Ibarra
Santo Domingo
Río Aguarico
QUITO
Cabo Pasado
Chone
Quevedo
Río Tiputini
Manta
Portoviejo
Cabo San Lorenzo
Jipijapa
Río Tigre
Río Corrientes

58

Ríohacha
nta Marta   Maicao
Pico
Cristóbal
Colón 5775m
Maracaibo
edupar
Machiques
San Carlos
del Zulia
Ocaña
Cúcuta
San Cristóbal
Pamplona
Bucaramanga
Duitama
Sogamoso
Tunja
Yopal
BOGOTÁ
Villavicencio
San José del Guaviare
La Chorrera
Iquitos

Golfo de
Venezuela
Lago
de
Maracaibo
Serranía de Perijá
Llanos
Río Casanare
Río Meta
Río Pauto
Río Apure
Río Arauca
Río Capanaparo
Puerto Miranda
San Fernando
de Apure
Río Tomo
Río Vichada
Río Manacacías
Río Guaviare
Río Inírida
Río Guainía
Río Negro
Río Içana
Río Yarí
Río Ajajú
Río Vaupés
Río Caquetá
Río Apaporís
Río Igara Paraná
Río Putumayo
Río Amazonas

OLOMBIA

CITY FOCUS: BOGOTÁ

Status: Capital of Colombia
Population: 7.4 million
Official language: Spanish
Founded: 1538
Currency: Colombian peso
Landmark: The BD Bacatá skyscraper, the country's highest building, 216 m (709 ft) tall

La Candelaria
area of Bogotá

South American jaguars, big cats up to 1.9 m (6.2 ft) long, live on the Llanos.

These green berries will turn red as they ripen.

Growing Coffee

Coffee is made from roasted coffee beans, which are the seeds of berries from *Coffea* shrubs. These shrubs are native to Africa, but are now grown in tropical regions worldwide. Coffee beans contain caffeine, which makes people feel wide awake. Colombia produces more than 750,000 tonnes (825,000 tons) of coffee beans every year—the weight of more than 400,000 family cars.

DID YOU KNOW? Colombia takes its name from Italian explorer Christopher Columbus, whose voyage of 1492 made Europeans aware of the American continent.

Ecuador

Ecuador takes its name from the equator, which runs to the north of the capital, Quito. The rain forest in the east, and the grasslands in the west, have a tropical climate with hot weather all year. In the central Andes Mountains, it is far cooler, with snow on the highest peaks.

Avenue of the Volcanoes

Down the middle of Ecuador are two lines of volcanoes, including nine over 5,000 m (16,400 ft) high. The volcanoes were formed by the same tectonic plate movement that made the Andes. The pressure melted rock inside the Earth. The liquid rock rose toward the surface, sometimes pouring from holes in the Earth's crust as lava.

Cab

Punt

Like all volcanoes, Illiniza Sur, Illiniza Norte, and Corazón are made from hardened lava.

The Galápagos Islands

Ecuador's Galápagos Islands are in the Pacific Ocean, 1,400 km (870 miles) west of Quito. It was after studying the animals on the different islands that Charles Darwin (1809–82) came up with his theory of evolution, which explains how living things change over time.

Galapágos Islands

Isla Pinta

Isla Marchena

Isla Fernandina

Isla San Salvador

Isla Isabela

Isla Santa Cruz

Isla Santa Fé

Isla San Cristóbal

Isla Santa María

Isla Española

Darwin noticed how the giant tortoises on each Galápagos Island have evolved to have differently shaped shells and necks so they can eat the different plants on each island.

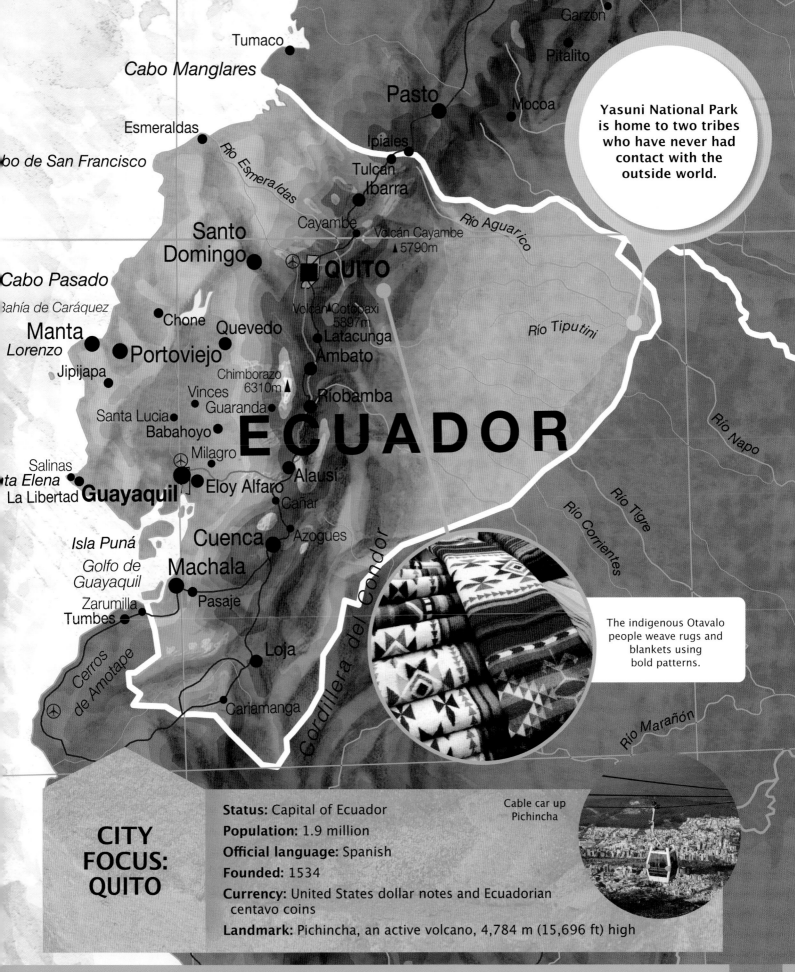

Tumaco

Cabo Manglares

Esmeraldas

bo de San Francisco

Pasto

Mocoa

Garzón

Pitalito

Ipiales

Tulcán

Ibarra

Río Esmeraldas

Cayambe

Río Aguarico

Volcán Cayambe
▲5790m

Santo
Domingo

QUITO

Río Tiputini

Cabo Pasado

Bahía de Caráquez

Chone

Quevedo

Volcán Cotopaxi
5897m

Latacunga

Manta

Lorenzo

Portoviejo

Ambato

Jipijapa

Chimborazo
6310m ▲

Vinces

Riobamba

Santa Lucia

Guaranda

Babahoyo

ECUADOR

Río Napo

Milagro

Salinas

ta Elena

La Libertad **Guayaquil**

Eloy Alfaro

Alausí

Cañar

Río Tigre

Río Corrientes

Isla Puná

Cuenca

Azogues

Golfo de
Guayaquil

Machala

Cordillera del Condor

Zarumilla

Tumbes

Pasaje

Cerros
de Amotape

Loja

Cariamanga

The indigenous Otavalo people weave rugs and blankets using bold patterns.

Río Marañón

**CITY
FOCUS:
QUITO**

Cable car up
Pichincha

Status: Capital of Ecuador

Population: 1.9 million

Official language: Spanish

Founded: 1534

Currency: United States dollar notes and Ecuadorian centavo coins

Landmark: Pichincha, an active volcano, 4,784 m (15,696 ft) high

DID YOU KNOW? Since the Earth bulges at the equator, the top of Ecuador's Mount Chimborazo is 2,163 m (7,096 ft) farther from Earth's core than the summit of Mount Everest.

Peru

Most of Peru's towns and cities are in the dry, flat coastal region, where many people work in factories, fishing, tourism, and farming. To the east of the Andes is the Amazon Rain Forest, covering more than half the country's area but home to only one in twenty Peruvians. Many of Peru's indigenous peoples live in the rain forest.

Cabo Pasado
Bahía de Caráquez
Manta
Cabo San Lorenzo
Portoviejo
Quevedo
Chimborazo 6310m
Babahoyo
Punta Santa Elena
Guayaquil
Eloy Alfaro
Golfo de Guayaquil
Cuenca
Machala
Tumbes
Cerros de Amotape
Punta Pariñas
Talara
Sullana
Piura
Castilla
Bahía de Sechura
Punta Negra
Desierto de Sechura
Isla Lobos de Tierra
Islas Lobos de Afuera
Chiclayo
Trujillo
Islas de Guañape
Chimbote
Punta Salino

The Inca Empire

From the 13th century until the arrival of the Spanish in the 16th century, the Incas ruled over an empire that stretched from southern Ecuador to Chile. The Incas constructed great stone buildings and had a network of paved paths through the mountains. To carry messages, they made different numbers of knots in strings that were linked together in a device called a *quipu*.

The Incas built homes, temples, and warehouses at Machu Picchu, high in the Andes Mountains.

CITY FOCUS: LIMA

Status: Capital of Peru

Population: 8.9 million

Official languages: Spanish, Quechua, and Aymara

Founded: 1535

Currency: Sol

Landmark: Lima Cathedral, built in 1649

Ceviche, made from spiced raw fish cured in lemon juice

DID YOU KNOW? Every year, Peruvians eat around 65 million guinea pigs, which are native to the Andes Mountains.

Lake Titicaca

The largest lake in South America, Lake Titicaca lies on the border between Peru and Bolivia. It has an area of 8,372 sq km (3,232 sq miles). The Uros indigenous people use reeds to build floating islands on the lake. The Uros live on the islands, fishing and catching waterbirds to eat.

Centuries ago, the Uros moved onto the lake to escape attack. Today, many islands still have watchtowers.

Cusco was the capital of the Inca Empire, with palaces, temples, and wide avenues.

Llamas are kept for carrying loads and for their wool, meat, and milk.

ADOR

PERU

Volcán Cayambe
5790m
Cotopaxi

Rio Tiputini

Rio Corrientes

Rio Igara Paraná

Iquitos

Rio Amazonas

Rio Curicurian

Rio Negro

Rio Itui

Rio Ucayali

Tarapoto

Cerros de Sierra de Canchyuaya

Rio Ucayali

Pucallpa

Rio Tarauacá

Rio Envira

Nevado de Huascarán 6768m

Huaraz

Sierra de Divisor

Huánuco

Cerro de Pasco

Rio de las Piedras

Huaral

Huaral
Chosica
Ilao
Vitarte
LIMA

Huancayo

Rio Mantaro

Cordillera Urubamba

Rio Madre de Dios

Nevado Citac 5329m

Cordillera Vilcabamba

Cordillera Oriental

Ayacucho

Nevado Salpantay 6271m

Chincha Alta
Pisco

Cusco

Nevado Ausangate 6094m

Cordillera de Carabaya

Punta Carreta

Ica

Abancay

Pampa de Huayuri

Cerrro Chaucahuana 5105m

Nevado Salluyo 5999m

Nevado Coropuna 6425m

Nevado Coloio 5015m

Punta Parada

Juliaca

Puno

Lake Titicaca

Nevado Chachani 6075m

Volcán El Misti 5822m

Rio Camaná

Arequipa

Tambo

Volcán Tutupaca 5751m

Punta de Coles

Nevado Sajama 6542m

Oruro

Tacna

Arica

Brazil

With an area of 8.5 million sq km (3.3 million sq miles), Brazil is South America's largest country. When the Portuguese claimed the area in 1500, it was home to around 7 million people, including the Tupi, Guarani, and Arawak. Today, Brazil has 210 million inhabitants, most of them living along the coast and in the south.

The Amazon Rain Forest

Around 60 percent of the Amazon Rain forest lies in Brazil, covering its northwest. It is the world's largest tropical rain forest, where warmth and lots of rain allow 390 billion trees to grow tall and close together. One out of every ten of the world's animal and plants species are found here.

The call of the red-handed howler monkey can be heard for up to 5 km (3 miles) in the Brazilian Amazon.

Carnival

In the days before Lent, the period when Christians give up meat, Brazilians celebrate the festival of Carnival (from the Latin for "remove meat"). The cities organize parades, where people wear bright costumes and play music.

Carnival paraders often dance to samba music, which developed from the music of African slaves.

Nieuw Amsterdam
PARAMARIBO
St-Laurent-du-Moroni
Cayenne
NAME
Juliana Top
1230m
Oiapoque
L A N D S
Amapá

Macapá
Amazon
(Amazonas)
Ilha de
Marajó
Belém
idos
Santarém
ajos
Iriri
Itaituba
São
Luís
Parnaíba

Tocantins
Maraba
Imperatriz
Caxias
Sobral
Fortaleza
Quixadá
Mossoró
Teresina
Campina
Grande
Natal
Juàzeiro
do Norte
João Pessoa
Caruarú
Olinda
Recife
Maceió

B R A Z I L
Paulistana
Palmas
Petrolina
Juàzeiro

Xingu
São Francisco
Feira de
Santana
Aracaju
Alagoinhas
Salvador
Jequié
Vitória da
Conquista
Itabuna
Belmonte

Brazil was named by the Portuguese after the many brazilwood trees along the coast, once used for making a red dye called brazilin.

A 38–m (125–ft) statue of *Christ the Redeemer* overlooks the city of Rio de Janeiro.

bá
donópolis
BRASÍLIA
Goiânia
Jataí
Ipameri
orumbá
Uberlândia
Uberaba
Belo
Horizonte
Caravelas
Governador
Valadares

São José do
Rio Preto
Ribeirão Preto
Juiz de
Fora
Vitória
Campos dos Goytacazes

Campo Grande
Bela Vista
Araçatuba
São
Paulo
Nova
Iguaçu
Niterói
Rio de Janeiro

GUAY
Paraná
Londrina
Maringá
Santo
André
Santos

Ciudad del
Este
o Peró
842m
Cascavel
Foz de Iguaçu
Curitiba
Itajaí
Pilar
Encarnación
Blumenau
Florianópolis
Posadas
Passo
Fundo
Lajes
ntes
Uruguay
Santa Maria
Caxias do Sul
São Leopoldo
Porto Alegre
Lagoa dos Patos
Uruguaiana
Canoas
Salto
Rivera
Pelotas
Paysandú
Rio Grande
Durazno
URUGUAY
Colonia del Sacramento
Δ Cerro Catedral
514m

Metropolitan
Cathedral

CITY
FOCUS:
BRASÍLIA

Status: Capital of Brazil

Population: 3 million

Official language: Portuguese

Founded: 1960, when the site was picked to become a central capital, instead of Rio de Janeiro

Currency: Real

Landmark: Metropolitan Cathedral, built in 1970

DID YOU KNOW? More than 20 percent of the Amazon Rain Forest has been cut down by farmers, loggers, and mining companies, putting over 2,000 forest animals at risk of extinction.

Bolivia

Bolivia is one of two countries that are landlocked, or without a coastline, in the Americas. Its lack of ports, as well as its landscape, which ranges from the Andes peaks to desert and rain forest, have made it one of the poorest countries in South America. Yet, today, Bolivia's wealth is growing due to its oil, metals, and textiles.

Salt Flat

The world's largest salt flat, the Salar de Uyuni, is in the Andes Mountains on the Altiplano plateau, a vast flat area of high ground. A salt flat is an area covered in salt and other minerals. Like all salt flats, the Salar de Uyuni formed in a desert where salty lakes evaporated, or turned to gas, in the sun.

The Salar de Uyuni covers 10,500 sq km (4,000 sq miles).

The temples of the ruined city of Tiwanaku were probably built from around 100 CE.

CITY FOCUS: LA PAZ

Status: Executive and legislative capital of Bolivia

Population: 790,000

Official languages: Spanish, plus 36 indigenous languages including Guarani, Aymara, and Quechua

Founded: 1548

Currency: Boliviano

Landmark: The Plurinational Legislative Assembly, where lawmakers meet

La Paz

Mining

The rock beneath Bolivia is rich with oil, natural gas, tin, silver, gold, iron, and lithium, which is used in batteries. There are 135,000 miners in Bolivia, but many more people work at transporting, processing, and selling the products.

Silver is mined at Potosí.

The Bañados del Izozog is a wetland, situated in a vast dip. It often provides the only water for this dry region's jaguars and tapirs.

DID YOU KNOW? At a height of 3,640 m (11,942 ft) in the Andes Mountains, La Paz is the highest capital city in the world.

Paraguay and Uruguay

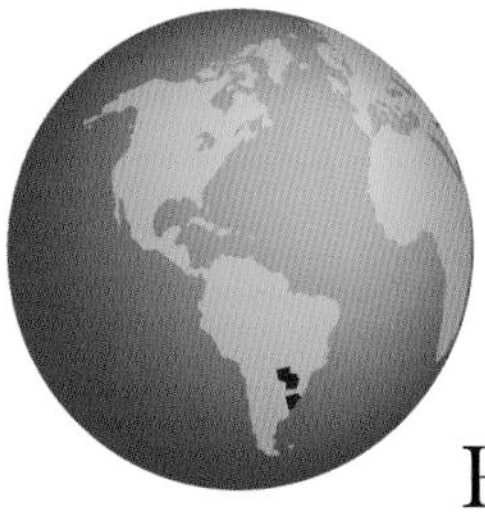

Paraguay's eastern region is covered by grassy plains and wooded hills, while to the west is a hot, dry plain known as the Chaco. Although landlocked, Paraguay has access to the sea along the Paraguay and Paraná Rivers, which reach the Atlantic Ocean at the southern border of Uruguay. Uruguay has a mild climate and a flat or gently hilly landscape.

The Itaipu Dam

On Paraguay's border with Brazil is the Itaipu Dam, completed in 1984. The 196 m/643 ft-high dam blocked the course of the Paraná River. Water is released through turbines, making them spin. Generators turn this energy into electricity. The dam provides four-fifths of Paraguay's electricity and a quarter of Brazil's.

The Itaipu Dam created a reservoir with an area of 1,350 sq km (520 sq miles).

Peñarol (left) and Club Nacional (right) are among South America's most successful soccer teams.

CITY FOCUS: MONTEVIDEO

Status: Capital of Uruguay

Population: 1.7 million

Official language: Spanish

Founded: 1724

Currency: Uruguayan peso

Landmark: Telecommunications Tower, the highest building in the country, 158 m (518 ft) tall

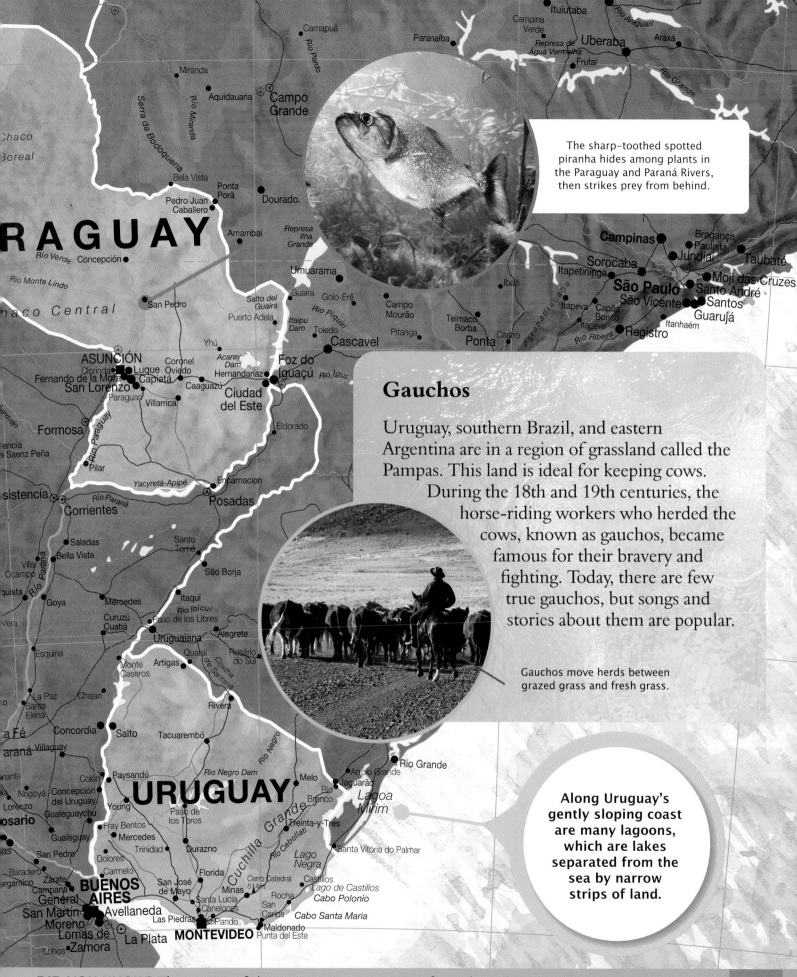

PARAGUAY

Chaco Boreal

Chaco Central

Chaco Central

The sharp–toothed spotted piranha hides among plants in the Paraguay and Paraná Rivers, then strikes prey from behind.

Serra da Bodoquena

Rio Verde · Concepción
Rio Monte Lindo

San Pedro

ASUNCIÓN
Clorinda
Fernando de la Mora · Luque · Capiatá
San Lorenzo
Paraguarí
Villarrica

Formosa

Rio Paraguay

Pilar

encia
Saenz Peña

sistencia
Corrientes

Rio Paraná

Saladas
Bella Vista
Villa
Ocampo
quista
Goya

Vera

Esquina

La Paz
Santa Elena
Chajarí

a Fé
Concordia · Salto
araná Villaguay
nante
Colón · Paysandú
Nogoyá
Lorenzo Concepción del Uruguay/
osario Gualeguaychú
Gualeguay
San Pedro
Baradero Zárate
ergamino Campana
General Martín
San Martín·
Moreno
Lomas de
Zamora
Lobos

Camapuã

Miranda
Aquidauana

Rio Miranda

Campo Grande

Bela Vista
Ponta
Porã
Pedro Juan
Caballero
Dourado

Amambaí

Represa
Ilha
Grande

Umuarama

Guaíra
Salto del
Guairá Goio-Erê
Puerto Adela
Itaipú Campo
Yhú Dam Mourão
Acaray Toledo
Dam
Coronel Foz do
Oviedo Iguaçú
Hernandariaz Rio Igue
Caaguazú
Ciudad Eldorado
del Este

Rio Pardo

Paranaíba

Rio Piquiri

Cascavel

Santo Tomé

São Borja

Itaquí
Rio Ibicuí
Curuzú Paso de los Libres
Cuatiá
Uruguaiana
Alegrete
Mercedes
Quaraí Rosário
Artigas do Sul
Monte
Caseros

Rivera

Tacuarembó

Rio Negro

Rio Negro Dam

URUGUAY

Young Paso de
los Toros
Fray Bentos
Mercedes
Gualeguay Trinidad Durazno
Dolores
Carmelo Florida
BUENOS
AIRES San José
de Mayo Minas
Avellaneda Santa Lucía
Las Piedras Canelones
La Plata **MONTEVIDEO** Pando
Punta del Este
Maldonado

Cuchilla Grande

Rio Negro
Melo
Jaguarão Rio
Branco
Lagoa
Mirim
Treinta-y-Tres
Rio Cebollati
Lago
Negra

Cerro Catedral
514m Castillos
Rocha Lago de Castillos
San Cabo Polonio
Carlos
Cabo Santa María

Arroio Grande
Rio Grande

Santa Vitória do Palmar

Campina
Verde Ituiutaba

Uberaba
Araxá
Represa de
Água Vermelha
Frutal

Rio Araguari

Rio Grande

Campinas Bragança
Paulista
Sorocaba Jundiaí Taubaté
Itapetininga
Ibati São Paulo Moji das Cruzes
São Vicente Santo André
Itapeva Capão Santos
Telmaco Bonito Guarujá
Pitanga Borba Itapeva Itanhaém
Ponta Castro Registro
Rio Ribeira

Gauchos

Uruguay, southern Brazil, and eastern Argentina are in a region of grassland called the Pampas. This land is ideal for keeping cows. During the 18th and 19th centuries, the horse-riding workers who herded the cows, known as gauchos, became famous for their bravery and fighting. Today, there are few true gauchos, but songs and stories about them are popular.

Gauchos move herds between grazed grass and fresh grass.

Along Uruguay's gently sloping coast are many lagoons, which are lakes separated from the sea by narrow strips of land.

DID YOU KNOW? The names of these countries may come from the indigenous Guarani language, with Paraguay meaning "mighty river" and Uruguay meaning "river of the bird."

69

Chile and Argentina

Long, thin Chile lies between the Andes Mountains and the Pacific Ocean. Argentina, covering 2.8 million sq km (1 million sq miles), is South America's second largest country. Both countries have climates ranging from hot and dry in the north to icy and windswept in the south.

The Iguazu Falls are the world's largest group of waterfalls, with a width of 2.7 km (1.7 miles).

Easter Island

Chile's Easter Island is in the Pacific Ocean, 3,500 km (2,170 miles) from the mainland. Between 1100 and 1680, the island's inhabitants carved more than 800 giant statues, called *moai*. They show the islanders' ancestors, who watch over their land and people.

Easter Island (Rapa Nui) (Chile)

Isla Sala y Gómez

The *moai* are around 4 m (13 ft) tall.

Tango dancing developed here in the 19th century.

CITY FOCUS: BUENOS AIRES

Status: Capital of Argentina

Population: 2.9 million

Official language: Spanish

Founded: 1536

Currency: Argentine peso

Landmark: Obelisk of Buenos Aires, a stone pillar 71.5 m (235 ft) tall, erected in 1936 to mark 400 years since the city's founding

Arequipa
Mollendo
Nevado Sajama 6542m
Arica
Pisagua
Iquique
Tocopilla
Mejillones
Antofagasta
Santa Catalina
Chañaral
Copiapó
Vallenar
La Serena
Ovalle
Cerro
Aconcagua
6962m
Viña del Mar
Valparaíso
San Bernardo
San Fernando
Talca
Parral
Chillán
Talcahuano
Concepción
Lebu
Los Angeles
Temuco
Valdivia
Osorno
Puerto Montt
Ancud
Isla de Chiloé

LA PAZ
Cochabamba
Santa Cruz
SUCRE
Potosí
Oruro 5995m
Ollagüe
Calama
Baquedano
La Quiaca
San Salvador de Jujuy
Salta
Ojos del Salado 6908m
San Miguel de Tucumán
Resistencia
Santiago del Estero
Catamarca
Deán Funes
San Juan
Córdoba
Mendoza
Rosario
Río Cuarto
Rancagua
San Rafael

BOLIVIA
Rondonópolis
Goiânia
Jataí
Ipameri
Corumbá
Uberlândia
Uberaba
São José do Rio Preto
Ribeirão Preto
Araçatuba

Montes Claros
Caravelas
Belo Horizonte
Governador Valadares

Gran Chaco
Puerto Sastre
Concepción
Embarcación
Campo Grande
Bela Vista

PARAGUAY
ASUNCIÓN
Formosa
Cerro Peró 842m
Pilar
General Pinedo
Corrientes
Santa Fé
Paraná
Mercedes

Londrina
Maringá
Cascavel
Foz de Iguaçu
Ciudad del Este
Encarnación
Passo Fundo
Posadas
Santa Maria
Uruguaiana
Canoas
Concordia
Salto
Rivera
Paysandú
Durazno

BUENOS AIRES
Avellaneda
Lomas de Zamora
La Plata
MONTEVIDEO
Río de la Plata
Cerro Catedral 514m

a Robinson Crusoe
SANTIAGO

ARGENTINA
Tandil
Maipu
Tres Arroyos
Necochea
Neuquén
Colorado
Bahía Blanca
Zapala
Choele Choel
Viedma
Golfo San Matías
Península Valdés
Punta Delgada
Puerto Madryn
Rawson
San Carlos de Bariloche
Esquel
Chubut
Las Plumas
Chico

HILE

D   E   L   O   S

Archipiélago de los Chonos
Puerto Aisén
Sarmiento
Colonia Las Heras
Deseado
Comodoro Rivadavia
Golfo de San Jorge
Fitz Roy
Puerto Deseado
Chico

Península de Taitao
Isla Wellington
Puerto Santa Cruz
Bahía Grande
Río Gallegos

Falkland Islands (Islas Malvinas) (U.K.)
West Falkland
Stanley
East Falkland

Archipiélago de la Reina Adelaida
Puerto Natales
Strait of Magellan
Punta Arenas
Isla Santa Inés
Isla Hoste
Isla Navarino
Isla Grande de Tierra del Fuego
Ushuaia
Isla de los Estados
Cape Horn

Patagonia

Pampas

Paraná
Uruguay
Paraguay
Pilcomayo
Paraná

Sixteenth-century European explorers hoped to find silver along the River Plata ("Silver River" in Spanish), giving Argentina its name, from the Latin *argentum* ("silver").

The Atacama Desert

The Atacama Desert, stretching for 1,000 km (600 miles) north to south, is in northern Chile. Moist air carried from the Pacific or Atlantic Oceans rises when it moves over the mountains that lie on both sides of the desert. As the moisture in the air cools, it condenses and falls as rain on the mountains, meaning that rain rarely reaches the desert.

The Atacama is one of the driest places on Earth, with around 1.5 cm (0.6 in) of rain per year.

DID YOU KNOW? Due to the many cattle farms on their grasslands, Argentinians eat more beef than anyone else, around 58 kg (129 lb) per person per year.

Atlantic Ocean

The world's second largest ocean covers more than 106 million sq km (41 million sq miles). It meets the Arctic Ocean in the north, the Southern Ocean in the south, the Pacific Ocean in the southwest, and the Indian Ocean in the southeast.

For the Christian festival of Santo Cristo, Azoreans decorate the streets with flowers.

The Mid-Atlantic Ridge

The world's longest mountain range runs for 16,000 km (10,000 miles) down the middle of the Atlantic Ocean. This ridge of rock was formed as tectonic plates moved apart from each other, letting magma rise to the surface between them. Several islands were made where the ridge rose above the water surface, including the Azores, St. Helena, and Tristan de Cunha.

The island country of Cape Verde became independent from Portugal in 1975.

With a population of 250, Edinburgh of the Seven Seas is the settlement on Tristan da Cunha, in the South Atlantic. It is 2,173 kilometres (1,350 miles) to the next settlement.

CITY FOCUS: ANGRA DO HEROÍSMO

Status: One of three capitals of the Azores region of Portugal

Population: 35,000

Official language: Portuguese

Founded: 1478

Currency: Euro

Landmark: Church of Mercy, built in 1746

Angra do Heroísmo

The map shows labels including:

NORWEGIAN SEA
ICELAND
Heimaey
Surtsey
NORWAY
FINLAND
SWEDEN
ESTONIA
DENMARK
NORTH SEA
LATVIA
LITHUANIA
UNITED KINGDOM
IRELAND
NETHER-LANDS
GERMANY
POLAND
LABRADOR SEA
NORTH ATLANTIC OCEAN
Newfoundland
FRANCE
São Jorge
Azores
Flores
Terceira
Pico
São Miguel
Santa Maria
PORTUGAL
SPAIN
CYPRUS
LEBANON
ISRAEL
MEDITERRANEAN SEA
JORDAN
Madeira
TUNISIA
MOROCCO
Lanzarote
La Palma
La Gomera
El Hierro
Tenerife
Islas Canarias
Gran Canaria
Fuerteventura
ALGERIA
CAPE VERDE
MAURITANIA
MALI
NIGER
SENEGAL
THE GAMBIA
BURKINA FASO
GUINEA-BISSAU
GUINEA
NIGERIA
SIERRA LEONE
CÔTE D'IVOIRE
GHANA
LIBERIA
CAMEROON
Penedos de São Pedro e São Paulo
Bioko
GULF OF GUINEA
Príncipe
EQUATORIAL GUINEA
SÃO TOMÉ AND PRÍNCIPE
São Tomé
Annobón
GABON
BRAZIL
Fernando de Noronha
Atol das Rocas
Ascension
Isla da Trindade
Ilhas Martin Vaz
St. Helena
SOUTH ATLANTIC OCEAN
PARAGUAY
URUGUAY
Rio de la Plata
Tristan da Cunha
Gough Island
Matías
Falkland Islands (Islas Malvinas)
East Falkland
Shag Rocks
South Georgia
Bouvetøya
South Sandwich Islands

The Mediterranean Sea

The Mediterranean Sea is often considered to be part of the Atlantic Ocean. A sea is a large area of saltwater that is smaller and less deep than an ocean.

The Sargasso Sea

The Sargasso Sea is an area of the North Atlantic Ocean where ocean currents leave the ocean plants they are carrying. Currents are great movements of water that are caused by differences in water temperature and saltiness. The area is named for its floating mats of sargassum seaweed.

Sargassum gives shelter and food to animals such as the sargassum fish.

DID YOU KNOW? The British island of Saint Helena, in the South Atlantic, was chosen as the prison for defeated French Emperor Napoleon (1769–1821) because it was so remote.

Asia

Asia is the largest continent by area and population. It covers 30 percent of Earth's land, around 44.5 million sq km (17.2 million sq miles). Asia is home to 4.6 billion people, making up 60 percent of the world's population. The largest country, Russia, and the most populous, China, are also here.

The Himalayas

The Himalaya mountains spread across parts of Afghanistan, Bhutan, China, India, Nepal, and Pakistan. The range started to form 50 million years ago, as the Indo-Australian tectonic plate moved into the Eurasian plate. This pushed and folded the rock upward, slowly making more than 50 mountains over 7,200 m (23,600 ft) high. The Himalayas are still growing by about 0.5 cm (0.2 in) a year.

The highest mountain in the world, the Himalayas' Mount Everest is 8,848 m (29,029 ft) high.

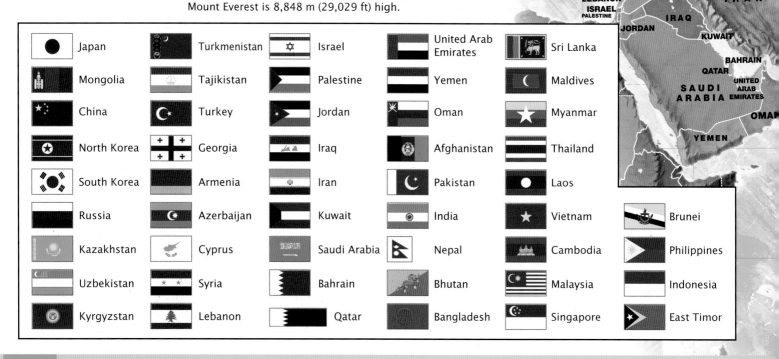

	Japan		Turkmenistan		Israel		United Arab Emirates		Sri Lanka
	Mongolia		Tajikistan		Palestine		Yemen		Maldives
	China		Turkey		Jordan		Oman		Myanmar
	North Korea		Georgia		Iraq		Afghanistan		Thailand
	South Korea		Armenia		Iran		Pakistan		Laos
	Russia		Azerbaijan		Kuwait		India		Vietnam		Brunei
	Kazakhstan		Cyprus		Saudi Arabia		Nepal		Cambodia		Philippines
	Uzbekistan		Syria		Bahrain		Bhutan		Malaysia		Indonesia
	Kyrgyzstan		Lebanon		Qatar		Bangladesh		Singapore		East Timor

DID YOU KNOW? There are over 30 megacities (cities with more than 10 million people) in Asia, more than in any other continent.

RUSSIA

AZAKHSTAN

MONGOLIA

KYRGYZSTAN

BEKI-
TAN
TAJIKISTAN

GHANISTAN

PAKISTAN

CHINA

NORTH
KOREA

SOUTH
KOREA

JAPAN

BHU

BANGLA-
DESH

INDIA

MYANMAR
(BURMA)

LAOS

THAILAND

VIETNAM

CAMBODIA

PHILIPPINES

SRI LANKA

MALDIVES

MALAYSIA

BRUNEI

SINGAPORE

INDONESIA

EAST
TIMOR

The Yangtze is the
world's third longest
river, after the
Amazon and Nile.

Yangtze River

Asia's longest river, the
Yangtze flows 6,300 km
(3,900 miles) across
China from west to east.
For thousands of years,
the river has offered fish,
transport, and drinking
water. It was in fields
watered by the Yangtze
that rice was first
planted, more than
8,000 years ago.

Japan

Japan is made up of 5 main islands—Hokkaido, Honshu, Kyushu, Shikoku, and Okinawa—and 6,847 smaller islands. More than 400 of Japan's islands are inhabited. The northern islands have long, snowy winters, while the islands of the far south have tropical rain forests. Japan is one of the wealthiest countries in the world, making popular products such as cameras, cars, computers, televisions, video games, and watches.

Kyoto

Japan's emperors ruled from the city of Kyoto for nearly 11 centuries, from 794 to 1869, when the royal court was moved to Tokyo. The city is home to several grand palaces, traditional gardens, and 2,000 temples. Around 1,600 of these temples are Buddhist, while the rest are Shinto shrines. These are Japan's two largest religions. Buddhism arrived in Japan from India in the 6th century. In Shintoism, which grew up in Japan, many god-like beings called *kami* are recognized. *Kami* may be the wind, rain, wisdom, poetry, or spirits of the dead.

NORTH KOREA

SOUTH KOREA

Uls

Pusa

Kita-Kyūs

Fukuoka

Kumamoto

Kyushu

Kagoshi

Ōsumi-shotō

Kyoto's Kinkaku–ji ("Temple of the Golden Pavilion") is a Buddhist temple set in a garden designed to seem like paradise.

N a n s e i - s h o t ō

Amami-Ō-sh

Every spring, people throughout Japan celebrate the beauty of cherry blossoms in the Hanami ("Flower Viewing") festival.

Okinawa-jima

DID YOU KNOW? Japan has one of the world's highest life expectancies, which is the average number of years people live: 84.5 years.

> Japan has 108 active volcanoes, including Mount Fuji, the tallest at 3,776 m (12,389 ft).

O. Kunashir
(Kunashiri-tō)

O. Iturup
(Etorofu-tō)

O. Shikotan
(Shikotan-tō)

These young macaques are bathing in a hot spring.

Sapporo

Hokkaidō

h'ŏngjin

ea of Japan
(East Sea)

Sendai

Oki-shotō

Honshū

TŌKYŌ
Hachiōji
Funabashi
Chiba
Fujisan
3776m
Kawasaki
Yokohama

Kyōto
Okayama
Osaka
Nagoya
Sakai
Kōbe
Hamamatsu

Hiroshima

Shikoku

J A P A N

Izu-shotō

Japanese Macaques

Japanese macaques live only in Japan. With their thick fur, they are able to live farther north than any other monkey. These are clever monkeys, and some wash their vegetables in the sea before eating. In winter, the macaques that live in Jigokudani Monkey Park warm themselves in hot springs, where the water has been heated by magma inside the Earth.

CITY FOCUS: TOKYO

Status: Capital of Japan

Population: 38.5 million

Official language: Japanese

Founded: 1457

Currency: Yen

Landmark: Tokyo Tower, built in 1958 to broadcast television signals, 333 m (1,092 ft) tall

Tokyo Tower

China, Mongolia, and the Koreas

The factories in China's many vast cities make more products than the factories of any other country. Like nearby North Korea, China is governed by Communist ideas, so business is carefully controlled by the government. North Korea is one of the world's poorest countries. In contrast, South Korea is one of the wealthiest, selling its telephones, TVs, and cars across the world.

Great Wall of China

The Great Wall's many sections stretch for 6,260 km (3,890 miles) across northwest China. Parts were built from the 7th century BCE, but most of what we see today was ordered by emperors of the Ming Dynasty (1368–1644). The wall was for keeping out enemies to the north and west.

The wall has watchtowers and, in many places, was wide enough for chariots to be driven along the top.

Gers have a wooden frame covered with woollen cloth.

Gers

One-third of Mongolians are nomadic, which means they move from grazing place to grazing place with their sheep, cows, goats, or horses. They carry their home, a round tent called a ger or yurt. Even in the capital city, Ulan Batar, some people live in gers.

DID YOU KNOW? North Korea has one of the largest armies in the world, employing 1.2 million people, which is nearly 5 out of every 100 citizens.

Many Korean dishes are made with noodles.

Hong Kong has 350 skyscrapers, more than any other city.

CITY FOCUS: BEIJING

The Forbidden City

Status: Capital of China

Population: 21.5 million

Official language: Mandarin Chinese

Founded: 1045 BCE

Currency: Renminbi (also called the "yuan")

Landmark: The Forbidden City, home to China's emperors from 1420 to 1912

Russia

Russia lies in both Asia and Europe. Around three-quarters of its population lives in the smaller, European portion. Northern Russia is covered by tundra and coniferous forest. To the south are wide expanses of grassland.

The city of St. Petersburg has 342 bridges.

Largest Lake

Lake Baikal in southern Russia is the world's largest freshwater lake. It contains 23,600 cubic km (5,670 cubic miles) of water, more than all the water in North America's Great Lakes. The lake was formed as two of Earth's tectonic plates moved apart from each other, creating a long, deep valley that is still widening. As a result, the area also has many large earthquakes, which can create tall waves on the lake.

Lake Baikal freezes over in winter.

The railway line was completed in 1916.

Longest Railway Line

The world's longest railway line, the Trans-Siberian Railway, crosses Russia from Moscow in the west to Vladivostok in the east. It is 9,289 km (5,772 miles) long, but also has many connecting lines with destinations such as China and Mongolia.

DID YOU KNOW? From 1922 to 1991, Russia was part of the Communist–ruled Union of Soviet Socialist Republics (USSR), which included 15 countries in northern Asia and eastern Europe.

Laptev
Sea

East Siberian
Sea

Chukchi
Sea

Bering
Sea

Kara
Sea

Zemlya Frantsa-Iosifa
(Franz Josef Land)

Ostrov
Komsomolets

Severnaya
Zemlya

Ark. Sedova

Ostrov
Bol'shevik

Ostrava
Komsomol'skoy
Pravdy

Ostrava Sergeya Kirova

Arkhipelag Nordenshel'da

Ostrava Izvestiy Tsik

Ostrava
Institута
Arkticheskogo

Poluostrov Taymyr

Novosibirskiye Ostrava

Ostrov Arzhu
Ostrov
Fadeyevskiy

Lyakhovskiye Ostrava

Ostrov
Novaya
Sibir'

Ostrov Bol'shoy
Lyakhovskiy

Ostrava Zhokhova

Ostrava
Mechenyy'i

Ostrova
Dunay

Ostrava
Kotel'nyy

Ostrov
Vrangelya

St. Lawrence
Island

St Matthew
Island

Pribilof Islands

Andyrskiy
Zaliv

Mys Navarin

Magadan

Kamchatka

Ostrov Karaginskiy

Oktyabr'skiy

Sakhalin

Sea of
Okhotsk

Okhotsk

Shantarskiye
Ostrava

Yakutsk

Khrebet
Cherskogo

Stanovoy Khrebet

Yablonovyy Khrebet

Noril'sk

Yenisey

Tura

Nizhnyaya Tunguska

Ust' Ilimsk

Lena

Oktyabr'skiy

Amur

Komsomol'sk

Khabarovsk

Tomsk

Achinsk

Kansk

Bratsk

Anzhero-Sudzhensk

Krasnoyarsk

Novosibirsk

Kemerovo

Leninsk-Kuznetskiy

Kiselevsk

Novokuznetsk

Mezhdurechensk

Abakan

Barnaul

Biysk

Rubtsovsk

Vostochnyy Sayan

Usol'ye-
Sibirskoye

Angarsk

Irkutsk

Ozero Baykal

Ulan-Ude

Manzhouli

ULAN
BATOR

Altai Mts

Ürümqi

mak

Jygonhan

R   U   S   S   I   A

Siberia is the name for the three-quarters of Russian land that lies in Asia.

At 4,750 m (15,580 ft), Klyuchevskaya Sopka is the highest active volcano in Asia.

Sea of Japan
(East Sea)

CITY FOCUS: MOSCOW

Status: Capital of Russia

Population: 17 million

Official language: Russian

Founded: 1147

Currency: Russian ruble

Landmark: The nine-domed St. Basil's Cathedral, built in 1561

St. Basil's
Cathedral

Central Asia

Five countries lie between the Caspian Sea in the west and China in the east: Kazakhstan, Kyrgyzstan, Tajikistan, Turkmenistan, and Uzbekistan. The climate here is dry, with hot summers and cool winters. Many people work in farming, mining, and manufacturing. While most people are Muslims, up to a quarter of the population are Christians.

The Silk Road

Samarkand's Registan square was built between 1417 and 1660.

The Silk Road was a network of routes used by traders for around 2,000 years from the 2nd century BCE. The main routes connected East and South Asia with the Middle East and Europe. Historians named the routes after one of its most valuable goods, Chinese silk. Cities in Central Asia that were along the Silk Road, such as Bukhara and Samarkand in Uzbekistan, became very wealthy. Religions such as Islam and Christianity, as well as inventions like paper, were also carried along the Silk Road.

CITY FOCUS: NUR-SULTAN

Status: Capital of Kazakhstan

Population: 1 million

Official languages: Kazakh and Russian

Founded: 1830

Currency: Tenge

Landmark: The Golden Towers, built in 1998, on either side of the entrance to the president's palace

Golden Towers

DID YOU KNOW? About 70 percent of Turkmenistan's land is covered by the Karakum Desert, which gets no more than 15 cm (6 in) of rain per year.

Kamensk-Ural'skiy
Miass
Chelyabinsk
Kurgan
Jitamak
Petropavl
Omsk
Tomsk
Anzhero-Sudzhensk
Novosibirsk
Kostanay
Kökshetaū
Rüdnyy
Pavlodar
Ermak
Orsk
Rubtsovsk
NUR-SULTAN
Semey
Öskemen
Qaraghandy

Kazakhstan is the wealthiest Central Asian country because of its oil, natural gas, and minerals.

K A Z A K H S T A N

Zhezqazghan

Balqash
Balqash Köli

Taldyqorghan

Aral Sea

Qyzlorda
Syrdarya

Qizilqum

Around half of the people who live in Kyrgyzstan work in farming.

UZBEKISTAN
Urganch

Taraz
Almaty
BISHKEK
Ysyk-köl
KYRGYZSTAN
Shymkent
Tien shan
TASHKENT
Chirchiq
Ang'ren
Olmaliq
Qo'qon
Andijon
Osh
Navoiy
Jizzax
Khŭjand
Fargona
Bukhara
Samarkand
Qarshi
Türkmenabat
...STAN
Amudarya

DUSHANBE
TAJIKISTAN

Mazār-e Sharif

In Kyrgyzstan, competitors in Tyiyn Enmei try to pick up a token while galloping.

The flagpole at the president's palace in Dushanbe, Tajikistan, is 165 m (541 ft) high.

Brave Riders

It was probably in Central Asia that wild horses were first domesticated, or tamed, at least 5,000 years ago. The nomadic people of this region used horses for hunting, transport, and war. Today, fast and dangerous horse sports are very popular.

Turkey and the Caucasus

A small part of Turkey is on the Balkan Peninsula of Europe, but the rest covers the Anatolian Peninsula of Asia. To the east, in the Caucasus region between the Black and Caspian Seas, are the countries of Armenia, Azerbaijan, and Georgia.

Fairy Chimneys

In the Cappadocia region of central Turkey are many tall towers of rock, which are often called "fairy chimneys." They are made of a soft rock called tuff, which can be worn away into strange shapes by water and wind. When the region was part of the Roman Empire, Christians moved here to escape the Romans, who sometimes forced them to worship Roman gods. The Christians carved the chimneys into churches, homes, and storehouses.

Today, some of the chimneys are used as hotels and restaurants.

Istanbul's Hagia Sophia was built as a Christian cathedral in 537, later became a Muslim mosque, and is now a museum.

Simfero
Sevastop

B l a c

Black Sea

Zonguldak

İstanbul
Tekirdağ
Sakarya
Kara
İzmit (Körfez)
Balıkesir
Bursa
ANKA
Kütahya
Eşkisehir
Kırı
T U
Manisa
Uşak
Afyon
İzmir
Aydın
Denizli
Isparta
Ak
Konya
Antalya
Rodos
Al L
L

DID YOU KNOW? Azerbaijan has 350 mud volcanoes, which erupt mud heated inside the Earth rather than lava.

Sea

Sokhumi

Vladikavkaz

Grozny

Makhachkala

Caspian Sea

Kutaisi

GEORGIA

Bat'umi

TBILISI ■

Samsun

Trabzon

ARMENIA

Vanadzor

Gäncä

G. Bazardüzü dağ 4466m

Ordu

Bayburt

Kumairi (Gyumri')

G. Aragac 4090m

AZERBAIJAN ■ **BAKU**

YEREVAN

Sivas

Erzincan

Erzurum

Büyük Ağrı Dağı (Mt. Ararat) 5165m

RKEY

Kayseri

Elazığ

Van

Ardabīl

Rasht

Diyarbakır

Batman

Armenia has its own alphabet, with 39 letters.

Adıyaman

Gaziantep

Şanlı Urfa

Qazvīn

Karaj

na

Osmaniye

Kilis

Al Mawşil

skenderun

Hatay

Arbīl

iqīyah takia)

Dervishes whirl while listening to music.

ka

Whirling

The Mevlevi Sufis are a group of Muslims based in Turkey. Members of their group are called Dervishes. They believe that a way to understand God's perfection is to whirl round and round, while forgetting their own needs and focussing only on God.

The Middle East

This hot, dry region was probably named the "Middle East" by the British. Around 6,000 years ago, the world's first civilization began here, in the land watered by the Tigris and Euphrates Rivers, in modern Iraq. Today, the region is still of great importance, as home to major religions and large supplies of oil.

Birthplace of Religions

Judaism, Christianity, and Islam are monotheist religions (believing in one God), and all grew up in the Middle East. Judaism developed in the region of modern Israel from around 4,000 years ago. Just over 2,000 years ago, Christianity began among Jewish people who heard the teachings of Jesus. In 610 CE, in Mecca in modern Saudi Arabia, the Prophet Muhammad began to spread the word of Islam.

The city of Jerusalem, in Israel and Palestine, is holy to Jews, Christians, and Muslims.

CITY FOCUS: SANAA

Status: Capital of Yemen
Population: 3.9 million
Official language: Arabic
Founded: 2nd century BCE
Currency: Yemeni rial
Landmark: The tower houses of the Old City, built with stone and mud bricks from the 11th century

Tower houses

DID YOU KNOW? Qatar has the highest income per person of any country, thanks to its reserves of oil and natural gas, as well as its small population of just 2.6 million.

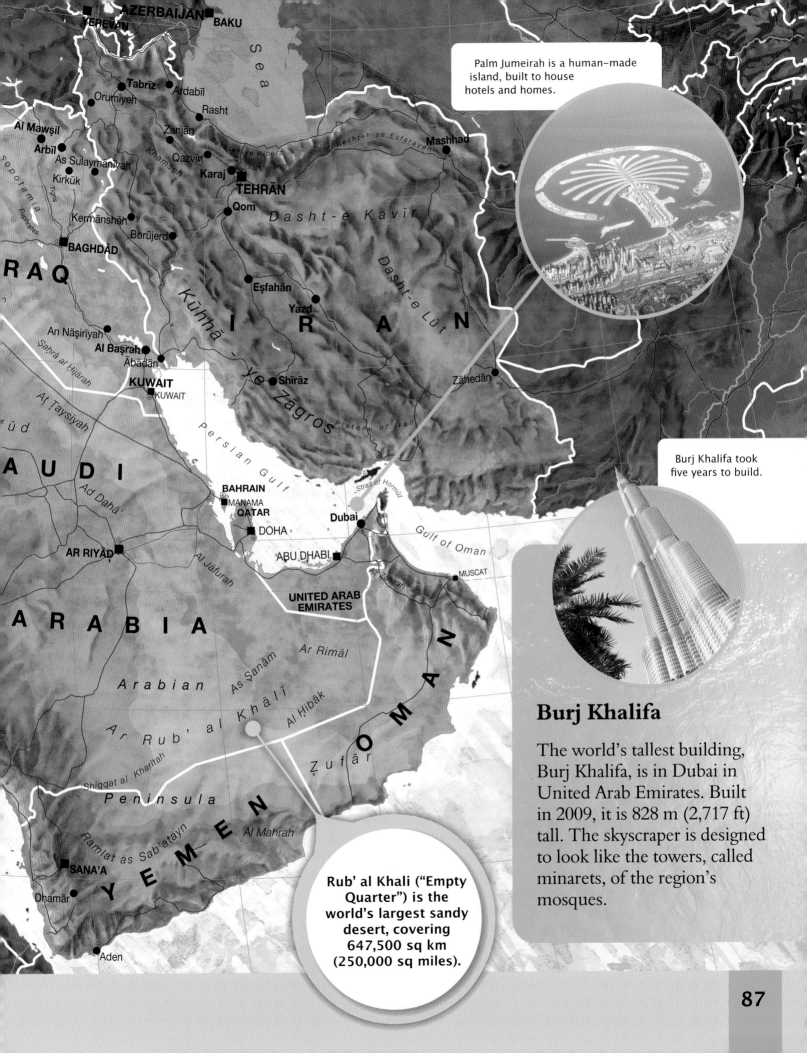

AZERBAIJAN
BAKU
YEREVAN

Sea

Tabrīz
Ardabīl
Orūmīyeh
Rasht
Al Mawṣil
Zanjān
Arbīl
Qazvīn
As Sulaymānīyah
Karaj
Kirkūk
TEHRĀN
Kermānshāh
Qom
BAGHDĀD
Borūjerd

RAQ

Dasht-e Kavīr

Eṣfahān

Dasht-e Lūt

I R A N

Yazd

An Nāṣirīyah
Al Baṣrah
Ābādān
KUWAIT
Shīrāz
KUWAIT
Zāhedān

Ṣaḥrā al Ḥijārah
AʈTaysīyah
ūd

Plateau of Iran

AUDI

Persian Gulf

Kūhhā-ye Zāgros

Strait of Hormūz

BAHRAIN
MANAMA
QATAR
Dubai

Ad Dahā'
DOHA
Gulf of Oman

AR RIYĀḌ
ABU DHABI
MUSCAT

Al Jafūrah
Aʈ Ẓāhirah

A R A B I A
UNITED ARAB
EMIRATES

Ar Rimāl

Arabian
As Sanām
Ar Rub' al Khālī
Al Ḥibāk

O M A N

Ar Rub' al Kharītah
Ẓufār

Shiqqat al Kharītah
Peninsula

Ramlat as Sab'atayn
Al Mahrah

SANA'A
Y E M E N

Dhamār

Aden

> Palm Jumeirah is a human–made island, built to house hotels and homes.

> Burj Khalifa took five years to build.

Burj Khalifa

The world's tallest building, Burj Khalifa, is in Dubai in United Arab Emirates. Built in 2009, it is 828 m (2,717 ft) tall. The skyscraper is designed to look like the towers, called minarets, of the region's mosques.

> Rub' al Khali ("Empty Quarter") is the world's largest sandy desert, covering 647,500 sq km (250,000 sq miles).

South Asia

Most of South Asia experiences the monsoon, when winds blowing over the Indian Ocean bring heavy rain from July to September. The monsoon gives much needed water to crops, but can cause life-threatening floods. In the south of the region, it is hot all year. The temperature falls as the Himalayas rise in the north.

Hinduism

Hinduism developed in India after around 500 BCE, growing from beliefs that had taken shape over thousands of years. Hindus believe in a God, called Brahman, who is everywhere and inside everyone. God can take many forms, which some Hindus worship as separate gods and goddesses. Hindus believe in reincarnation—that each living thing's soul lives many times, in one human body, animal, or plant after another.

From around 3300 BCE, the Indus Valley was home to a great civilization. People lived in neatly ordered cities, where homes had toilets from which waste was washed into underground sewers.

The Hindu festival of Holi takes place every spring. People throw bright powders over each other to celebrate the start of spring and the triumph of good over evil. Holi is one of the most popular festivals among the 1 billion Hindus in India, as well as the 100 million who live in the rest of South Asia and around the world.

Along the coast of Sri Lanka, fishermen perch on crossbars of tall poles.

Map labels

AFGHANISTAN
KĀBUL
Kandāhār
Quetta
PAKISTAN
Karachi
Indus
Hyderābād
Jodhp
Rajkot
Valsad
Silvassa
Thane
Mumbai
Pune (Poon
Panaji
Mang (Manga
Laccadive Islands
Amindivi Islands
Kavaratti
Kozhiko
Koyamutth
Cannanore Islands
Thi
Thiladunma
MALDIVES

CITY FOCUS: KATHMANDU

Status: Capital of Nepal

Population: 1.7 million

Official language: Nepali

Founded: 723

Currency: Nepalese rupee

Landmark: Durbar Square, home to palaces and Buddhist and Hindu temples

Kathmandu

At 120 km (75 miles) long, Cox's Bazar is the longest natural sea beach in the world.

The Taj Mahal

The Taj Mahal, in the city of Agra, in India, was built between 1632 and 1653. It was ordered by Emperor Shah Jahan as a tomb for his beloved wife, Mumtaz Mahal. Shah Jahan's empire covered much of modern India, Pakistan, Afghanistan, and Bangladesh.

The Taj Mahal is built from white marble.

DID YOU KNOW? In 1999, the Bhutanese government allowed television and the internet for the first time, but warned citizens against overusing the technologies.

89

Mainland Southeast Asia

On the Indochinese Peninsula, which juts into the Bay of Bengal and South China Sea, are the countries of Myanmar, Thailand, Laos, Cambodia, and Vietnam. Most of this region is hot and rainy, which is a good climate for growing rice. In the northern mountains, winters can be cold.

Angkor Wat

The temple of Angkor Wat, in Cambodia, was built as a Hindu temple in the 12th century. Later that century, it was turned into a Buddhist temple. Today, around 95 percent of Cambodians are Buddhists. Angkor Wat was designed to symbolize Mount Meru, a holy mountain in the stories of Hinduism and Buddhism. The towers symbolize the five peaks of Meru, while the walls and moat represent the surrounding mountains and ocean.

With a moat more than 5 km (3 miles) long, Angkor Wat is one of the biggest temples in the world.

MY
(E

Monywa

Sittwe   Minbu

NAYPYIL

Ramree

Thandwe

Hinthada

Bassein **Ran**

Cape Negrais

Coco
Islands

Andaman
Islands

A.

CITY FOCUS: BANGKOK

Status: Capital of Thailand
Population: 8.3 million
Official language: Thai
Founded: 15th century
Currency: Baht
Landmark: The Grand Palace, used by
 Thai kings since 1782

Floating market

Nicobar
Islands

Descending Dragon

Vietnamese legends say that Ha Long Bay was made by a family of dragons (Ha Long means "Descending Dragon"). The dragons spat out jewels, which turned into rocks and islands.

Ha Long Bay is actually made from limestone rock that has been worn away.

Most people in Laos live in the valleys around the Mekong River.

MYANMAR (BURMA)

Mandalay

Taung-gyi

Thaton

Hpaan
Moulmein

Tavoy

Beit
Kyunzu

Surat
Thani

Kota Bharu

Gejiu

Thai Nguyên

HANÔI

Haiphong

Thai Binh

Nam Dinh

Thanh Hoa

Ha Long

Qinzhou

Beihai

Zhanjiang

Mekong

Luang Prabang

L A O S

Chiang Mai

Lampang

VIENTIANE

Udon Thani

THAILAND

Nakhon Sawan

Nakhon Ratchasima

Ubon Ratchathani

Annam Highlands

Huê

VIETNAM

Quang Ngai

Qui Nhon

Tuy Hoa

Nha Trang

Cam Ranh

Ba Ngoi

Đalat

BANGKOK

Chon Buri

CAMBODIA

Mekong

PHNOM PENH

Gulf of Thailand

Long Xuyên

Mỹ Tho

Cân Tho

Rach Gia

Bien Hoa

Phan Thiêt

Ho Chi Minh

Mũi Cà Mau

South China Sea

On hillsides, rice is grown on flat terraces cut into the land.

DID YOU KNOW? Around 90 percent of the world's rubies are mined in Myanmar, along with sapphires and jade.

Islands of Southeast Asia

Six Asian countries share the 25,000 islands between mainland Asia and Australia: Brunei, Indonesia, Malaysia, Philippines, Singapore, and East Timor. The largest island, New Guinea, is divided between Indonesia and Papua New Guinea, which is part of Oceania.

Borobudur

The world's largest Buddhist temple is Borobudur, on Java, in Indonesia. Visitors walk a path that climbs through three worlds— the lowest, filled with need; a higher world, freed from need; and the heavenly world. The story is told by carvings. Buddhism is based on the teachings of Siddhartha Gautama, the Buddha, who lived in India some time in the 6th to 4th centuries BCE.

Borobudur was built in the 9th century.

Orangutans

Orangutans live in rain forest on Borneo and Sumatra, in Indonesia and Malaysia. They are at risk of extinction because of loss of their habitat.

Orangutans spend most of their time in trees, eating fruit.

Gulf of Thailand

Long Xuyên · Ho Chi Minh

Cần Thơ

Müi Cà Mau

M A L A Y S I

Malay Peninsula Malaya

Natuna Besar

Kepulauan Anambas

Kepulauan Natuna

Medan

Strait of Malacca

KUALA LUMPUR
PUTRAJAYA

Simeulu

Nias

SINGAPORE SINGAPORE
Bintan

Kepulauan Tambelan

Kepulauan Riau

Lingga

Kepulauan Lingga

Maya

Padang

Siberut

Kepulauan Mentawai

Sumatra

Bangka

Belitung

Palembang

Bandar Lampung

I

JAKARTA

Bandung Sen

Cimahi

Java Yogy

CITY FOCUS: SINGAPORE

Status: Capital and only city of Singapore
Population: 5.6 million
Official languages: English, Malay, Mandarin Chinese, and Tamil
Founded: 13th to 14th century
Currency: Singapore dollar
Landmark: The Supertree Grove

Up to 50 m (160 ft) tall, the Supertrees are home to vines and flowers, but also hold solar panels to make power.

The grass on the "Chocolate Hills" turns brown like chocolate in the dry season.

Seram Island has 117 species of birds, including the Seram masked owl, which lives nowhere else.

South China Sea

PHILIPPINES

Luzon

Catanduanes

MANILA ● Quezon City

Samar

Mindoro

Masbate

Busuanga
Calamian

Panay

Leyte

Cebu
Negros Cebu Bohol

Spratly Islands
(Truong Sa Islands)

Palawan

Sulu
Sea

Mindanao
Davao

Cape San
Augustin

Balabac

Zamboanga

Jolo

Kepulauan
Nanusa

Tawitawi

Sulu Archipelago

Celebes
Sea

Kepulauan
Karkaralong

Kepulauan
Talaud

BANDAR
SERI
BEGAWAN

Sabah

Kepulauan
Sangir

Morotai

BRUNEI

Sarawak

Minahassa Peninsula

Bacan

Halmahera

Waigeo

Doberai Peninsula

Numfoor

Biak

Yapen

Pegunungan Van Rees

Irian Jaya

New Guinea

Pegunungan Maoke

Kalimantan

Kepulauan
Togian

Peleng

Tanjung
Libobo

Obi

Ceram
Sea

Misoöl

Kepulauan
Balabalagan

Sulawesi

Taliabu

Buru

Maluku (Moluccas)

Seram

Wokam

Laut

Muna

Buton

Banda Sea

Makassar
(Ujung Pandang)

Kepulauan Barat Daya

I N D O N E S I A

Tanjung
Selatan

Wetar

Pegunungan Meratus

Java Sea

Madura

Flores
Sea

Lesser Sunda Islands

Kepulauan
Solor

Alor

DILI

EAST
TIMOR

Surabaya

Bali
Sea

Flores

Cape
Van

Malang

Bali

Lombok

Sumbawa
Tanjung
Karossa

Sumba

Rote

Timor
Sea

DID YOU KNOW? More people live on Java than on any other island in the world: 141 million, making up more than half of Indonesia's population of over 270 million.

Europe

Most of Europe has a mild climate, with warm summers and cool winters. However, the far north is cold year round, while the regions around the Mediterranean Sea have hot, dry summers. Three-quarters of Europe's people live in cities, where they work in industries from banking to fashion.

ICELAND

The Alps

The Alps are the highest and largest mountain range that lies completely in Europe. From west to east, the range curves across parts of France, Switzerland, Monaco, Italy, Liechtenstein, Austria, Germany, and Slovenia. The highest peak, Mont Blanc, crosses the French–Italian border, reaching 4,810 m (15,781 ft). In winter, the Alps are popular with skiers and snowboarders.

Deep valleys have been cut into the Alps by ice and rivers.

IRELAND

CELTIC SEA

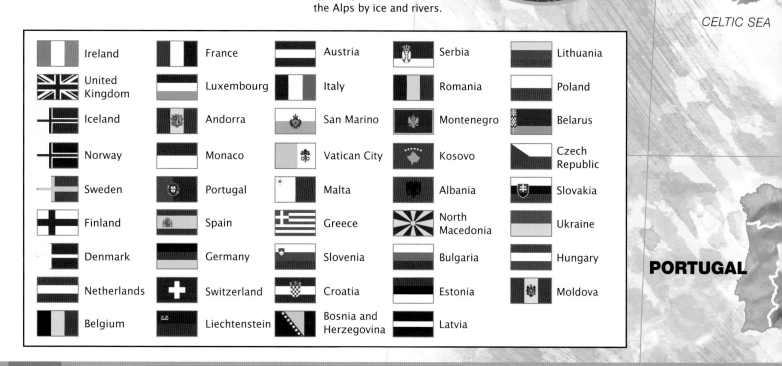

Ireland	France	Austria	Serbia	Lithuania
United Kingdom	Luxembourg	Italy	Romania	Poland
Iceland	Andorra	San Marino	Montenegro	Belarus
Norway	Monaco	Vatican City	Kosovo	Czech Republic
Sweden	Portugal	Malta	Albania	Slovakia
Finland	Spain	Greece	North Macedonia	Ukraine
Denmark	Germany	Slovenia	Bulgaria	Hungary
Netherlands	Switzerland	Croatia	Estonia	Moldova
Belgium	Liechtenstein	Bosnia and Herzegovina	Latvia	

PORTUGAL

NORWEGIAN SEA

Vestfjorden

NORWAY

Sognefjorden

Boknafjorden

SWEDEN

FINLAND

Gulf of Bothnia

Gulf of Finland

ESTONIA

DENMARK

NORTH SEA

Baltic Sea

LATVIA

LITHUANIA

UNITED KINGDOM

RUSSIA

NETHER-
LANDS

POLAND

BELARUS

GERMANY

nglish Channel

BELGIUM

LUXEMBOURG

CZECH
REPUBLIC

UKRAINE

SLOVAKIA

MOLDOVA

AUSTRIA

LIECHTENSTEIN

FRANCE SWITZERLAND

HUNGARY

ROMANIA

Sea of Azov

of Biscay

SLOVENIA

CROATIA

SAN
MARINO

BOSNIA &
HERZEGOVINA

SERBIA

MONACO

MONTENEGRO

BULGARIA

BLACK SEA

ANDORRA

ITALY

KOSOVO

Bosporus

VATICAN
CITY

NORTH
MACEDONIA

ALBANIA

PAIN

GREECE

MALTA

The Danube River

The Danube flows through 10 countries, more than any other river: Germany, Austria, Slovakia, Hungary, Croatia, Serbia, Bulgaria, Romania, Moldova, and Ukraine, where it empties into the Black Sea.

The Danube runs past the Hungarian Parliament in Budapest, the country's capital.

DID YOU KNOW? Belgium, Denmark, Liechtenstein, Luxembourg, Monaco, the Netherlands, Norway, Spain, Sweden, and the United Kingdom have a king or queen as head of state.

95

Britain and Ireland

The Republic of Ireland and United Kingdom lie on two big islands and 6,000 smaller ones off the northwestern coast of mainland Europe. The United Kingdom is made up of four countries: England, Northern Ireland, Scotland, and Wales. Common languages include English, Irish, Scots, Welsh, Polish, and Hindi.

Castles

The first stone castle on these islands, the Tower of London, was built in 1078. In the following centuries, thousands of high-walled castles were built by kings and lords to control their land and withstand attack. After the 17th century, when cannon fire could break down walls, castles no longer offered a form of protection, but many still stand today.

Harlech Castle in Wales was built on high ground to watch all around.

Ara

Erris Head

Done

Achill Island
Clew Bay

The Giant's Causeway

The Giant's Causeway, in Northern Ireland, is made of lava that ran out of a huge volcano. As the lava cooled, it cracked into 40,000 evenly shaped blocks, many of them hexagonal (with six sides).

A legend tells us the Giant's Causeway was built by the giant Finn MacCool.

Ireland's capital, Dublin, has a bridge shaped like the national symbol: the harp.

IRELAND
Galway
Galway Bay
Aran Islands

Lime

Dingle Bay

Com

Mizen Head   Cape Clear Island

CITY FOCUS: LONDON

Status: Capital of the United Kingdom

Population: 9.3 million

Official language: English

Founded: 47 CE

Currency: Pound sterling

Landmark: The Shard, the tallest building in the United Kingdom, 309.6 m (1,016 ft) tall

The Shard and Tower Bridge

North Rona
Sula Sgeir
Sule Skerry
Stack Skerry
Papa Westray
Westray
North Ronaldsay
Fair Isle
Sanday
Rousay
Stronsay
Mainland
Hoy
South Ronaldsay
Orkney Islands
Pentland Firth

Outer Hebrides
annan Isles
Butt of Lewis
Isle of Lewis
North Uist
South Uist
Barra
Rum
Eigg
Muck
Coll
Tiree
Iona
Colonsay
Islay
Jura
Mull
Skye
The Minch
Little Minch
Sea of the Hebrides
Firth of Lorn
Cape Wrath

Scotland
Inverness
Aberdeen
Moray Firth
Kinnairds Head

North Sea

UNITED

KINGDOM

These giant sculptures in Falkirk show kelpies, which are shape-changing creatures said to live in the waters of Scotland.

Perth
Dundee
Stirling
Alloa
Kirkcaldy
Fife Ness
Glasgow
Edinburgh
Firth of Forth
Paisley
Motherwell
Kilmarnock
Ayr
Arran
Sound of Jura
North Channel
Firth of Clyde

Malin Head
Rathlin Island
Londonderry
Ballymena
Northern Ireland
Lough Neagh
Bangor
Belfast
Strangford Lough

Dumfries
Carlisle
Solway Firth
Luce Bay

Blyth
Newcastle upon Tyne
South Shields
Sunderland
Hartlepool
Durham
Middlesbrough
Darlington
Workington
Whitehaven
Scarborough
Flamborough Head
Bridlington
Bridlington Bay

Dundalk
Dundalk Bay
Drogheda
Isle of Man
Barrow-in-Furness
Fleetwood
Blackpool
Lancaster
Harrogate
York
Preston
Blackburn
Halifax
Bradford
Leeds
Kingston upon Hull
Humber
Grimsby

Irish Sea

DUBLIN
Dún Laoghaire
Anglesey
Liverpool
Birkenhead
Colwyn Bay
Chester
Wrexham
Crewe
Stockport
Manchester
Bolton
Chesterfield
Sheffield
Lincoln
Stoke-on-Trent
Derby
Nottingham
Boston
The Wash

Caernarfon Bay

Stafford
Shrewsbury
England
King's Lynn

Cambrian Mountains
Cardigan Bay
Wales
Wolverhampton
Walsall
Leicester
Peterborough
Norwich
Great Yarmouth
Lowestoft
Dudley
Birmingham
Coventry
Severn
Cambridge
Bury St Edmunds
Ipswich

Waterford
Carnsore Point
St George's Channel
St David's Head

Great Malvern
Worcester
Hereford
Banbury
Northampton
Bedford
Cheltenham
Merthyr Tydfil
Rhondda
Newport
Gloucester
Thames
Oxford
Luton
Harlow
Colchester
Clacton-on-Sea
Chelmsford
Llanelli
Swansea
Cardiff
Bristol
Swindon
Slough
LONDON
Basildon
Southend-on-Sea
Barry
Weston-super-Mare
Bath
Reading
Windsor
Chatham
Ramsgate
Bristol Channel
Bridgwater
Basingstoke
Guildford
Canterbury
Dover
Brugge
Oostende
Dunkerque
Lundy
Taunton
Aldershot
Winchester
Crawley
Folkestone
Calais
tic Sea
Salisbury
Hastings
Cap Gris-Nez
Boulogne-sur-Mer
Bude Bay
Yeovil
Southampton
Worthing
Brighton
Bexhill
Eastbourne
Exeter
Weymouth
Bournemouth
Poole
Portsmouth
Plymouth
Lyme Bay
Portland Bill
Isle of Wight
Torquay
English Channel
Strait of Dover

At its narrowest, the Channel between England and France is 34 km (21 miles).

Land's End
Lizard Point
Start Point
Isles of Scilly

Alderney
Cap de la Hague
Cherbourg
Guernsey
CHANNEL ISLANDS (U.K.)
Sark
Jersey
Baie de la Seine
Dieppe
Le Havre
Bolbec
Rouen
Amiens
Beauvais
Caen
Évreux
Seine
PARIS

DID YOU KNOW? The United Kingdom has a national parliament, in London, England, while Northern Irish, Scottish, and Welsh parliaments make laws that affect their own regions.

97

Scandinavia

This region of northern Europe includes the countries of Denmark, Finland, Iceland, Norway, and Sweden. Northern Scandinavia extends into the icily cold Arctic Circle, but the south has warm summers. With many industries and natural resources, the Scandinavian countries are among the world's wealthiest.

N O

Glaciers

There are over 2,000 glaciers in this region. Glaciers are slow-moving rivers of ice. They form near the poles or on high mountains when snow falls faster than it can melt. As glaciers slide downhill, dragging rocks with them, they carve out valleys over thousands of years. Along the coast of Norway are many of these valleys that have flooded with seawater. They are called fjords.

ICELAND

REYKJAVÍK

Heimaey
Surtsey

Streymoy
Tórshavn

FØROYAR
Faroe Island
(Denmark)

The first permanent settlers in Iceland arrived in around 874 after sailing from Norway.

Norway's Svartisen Glacier is shrinking because of the rise in worldwide temperatures known as global warming.

The Svartsengi geothermal plant makes electricity, channels water for heating, and warms bathing pools.

Geothermal Energy

Geothermal energy is heat made inside the Earth. Beneath Iceland, tectonic plates are moving apart, melting rock and heating water that has soaked into the ground. Some of this hot water is diverted into pipes that heat 85 percent of Iceland's homes. Geothermal energy also makes a quarter of Iceland's electricity.

DID YOU KNOW? From the 8th to 11th centuries, Vikings from Norway, Denmark, and Sweden raided, traded, and settled around Europe and even as far as North America and North Africa.

NORWEGIAN SEA

Nordkapp

Sørøya

Lofoten Vesterålen

Vestfjorden

Inari-järvi

LAPPLAND

Cross-country skiing races, across flat or hilly ground, take place in winter.

NORWAY

Uddjaure

Umeälven

Oulu

Oulujärvi

Trondheim

Storsjön

Gulf of Bothnia

FINLAND

Päijänne

SWEDEN

Tampere

Lake Ladoga

Shetland Islands

Sognefjorden

Bergen

OSLO

Uppsala

Turku

HELSINKI

r Isle

Västerås

Åland

STOCKHOLM

Gulf of Finland

Boknafjorden

Stavanger

Vänern

Vättern

Gotland

Baltic Sea

Finland has at least 187,000 lakes, many of them in dips worn by ancient glaciers.

Göteborg

Öland

RIGA

LATVIA

DENMARK

Ålborg

NORTH SEA

Århus

Šiauliai

Klaipėda

LITHUANIA

COPENHAGEN

Malmö

Kaliningrad

Kaunas

Odense

Bornholm

RUSSIA

VILNIUS

Kiel

Gdańsk

CITY FOCUS: STOCKHOLM

Status: Capital of Sweden

Population: 1.6 million

Official language: Swedish

Founded: 1252

Currency: Krona

Landmark: Riddarholm Church, parts of it dating from the 13th century

Riddarholm Church and the Old Town

France, Belgium, and the Netherlands

These three countries are key members of the European Union, a group of around 27 countries that work together to make Europe safer and wealthier. Along France's borders are three microstates, or tiny countries: Luxembourg, Andorra, and Monaco. Andorra and Monaco are not European Union members, but they do use the shared European currency, the euro.

Monsters of Notre-Dame

Paris's cathedral of Notre-Dame was begun in 1160. The statues on the outside were carved to tell stories to the people of Paris, who usually could not read the Bible for themselves. There are statues of terrible monsters, some of them added later. These were warnings of the horrors believed to face those who led bad lives. In 2019, a fire destroyed the cathedral's spire. French people were divided between wanting to rebuild exactly as before and wanting to create something new.

This strix is a bird-like creature said to eat human flesh.

The Eiffel Tower

CITY FOCUS: PARIS

Status: Capital of France
Population: 10.4 million
Official language: French
Founded: 250–225 BCE
Currency: Euro
Landmark: The Eiffel Tower, built by engineer Gustave Eiffel in 1889, 324 m (1,063 ft) tall

Alde
Guernsey
CHANNEL ISLAND (U.K.) Je

Go

Île de Groix

Belle-Île

Île de Noirmout
Île d"Yeu

Bay of Biscay

Cabo de Ajo

Bilbao

The European Parliament meets in Brussels, Belgium, as well as in Strasbourg, France, to make laws that affect all countries in the European Union.

With a population of 614,000, Luxembourg is one of the smallest countries in Europe.

Digging Canals

The capital of the Netherlands, Amsterdam, has more than 100 km (60 miles) of canals. Most of the canals were dug in the 16th and 17th centuries. Connecting with the North Sea, which is part of the Atlantic Ocean, the canals brought goods across the city.

Many of Amsterdam's houses are tall and thin, to cram as many buildings along the canal front as possible.

Helgoland

NETHERLANDS

AMSTERDAM
THE HAGUE
Rotterdam
Utrecht
Neder Rijn
Waal

BERLIN

Antwerpen
Mönchengladbach

BRUXELLES
BELGIUM
Aachen

Wiesbaden

LUXEMBOURG
LUXEMBOURG

English Channel

Cap Gris-Nez

Cap de la Hague

Baie de la Seine

Seine
Marne
PARIS
Seine
Yonne

Moselle
Saar
Rhein
Strasbourg

Malo

Loire
Cher
Loire

F R A N C E
Saône

BERN

Lac Léman

Rhône

Gironde
Bordeaux
Dordogne
Garonne

Lyon

Torino

Toulouse
Garonne

Montpellier
Rhône

MONACO
Nice **MONACO**

Marseille

Côte d'Azur
Cap Camarat
Îles d'Hyères

Ligurian Sea
Cap Corse
Golfo de St-Florent

Corsica

ANDORRA
LA VELLA

Golfe du Lion

Cabo de Creus
Golf de Rosas

Costa Brava

Strait of Bonifacio

Zaragoza

Barcelona

DID YOU KNOW? Many people in the north of Belgium speak a form of Dutch, like they do in the Netherlands, while people in the south of the country usually speak French.

Spain and Portugal

Spain and Portugal are on the mountainous Iberian Peninsula. The most common languages here are Spanish, Portuguese, Catalan (spoken in northeastern Spain), and Galician (spoken in northwestern Spain). These all developed from the Latin spoken on the peninsula while it was ruled by Rome.

The Iberian wolf lives in northern Portugal and northwestern Spain.

Cabo Ortegal

Ferrol
A Coruña
Santiago de Compostela
Cabo Fisterra
Pontevedra
Vigo
Miño
Braga
Matosinhos Aveir
Ponto
Douro

PORTUGAL

Aveiro

Fairytale Architect

The Spanish architect Antoni Gaudí (1852–1926) designed many extraordinary buildings in the city of Barcelona, in the region of Catalonia. His buildings break many of the rules about how houses or churches should look. They seem to grow like trees, ripple like dragons' scales, or look just like a fairytale gingerbread house.

Coimbra

Tejo

Cabo da Roca
Amadora
Almada
Cabo Espichel

LISBON
Barreire
Setuba
Baía de Setúbal

Evo

The roof of Gaudí's Casa Battló is arched like the back of a writhing dragon.

Flamenco music is often performed on the guitar.

Flamenco

Flamenco is a style of music and dance that grew up in Andalusia, in southern Spain. Flamenco dancers stand proudly, use their arms to express strong emotion, and stamp their feet.

Cabo de São Vicente
Faro

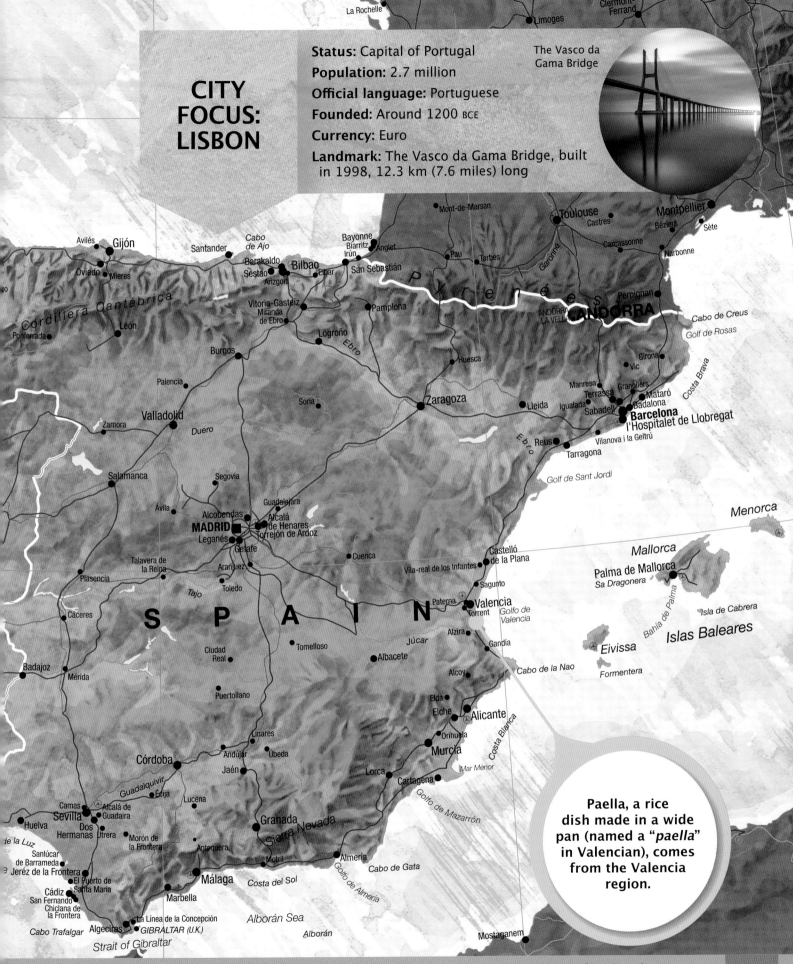

CITY FOCUS: LISBON

Status: Capital of Portugal
Population: 2.7 million
Official language: Portuguese
Founded: Around 1200 BCE
Currency: Euro
Landmark: The Vasco da Gama Bridge, built in 1998, 12.3 km (7.6 miles) long

The Vasco da Gama Bridge

Paella, a rice dish made in a wide pan (named a "*paella*" in Valencian), comes from the Valencia region.

DID YOU KNOW? Portugal produces two-thirds of the world's cork, the bark of cork oak trees, which is used in bottle stoppers and in insulation, to stop heat escaping from buildings.

Germany, Austria, and Switzerland

German is the official language of Germany and Austria, as well as one of the languages of Switzerland, alongside French, Italian, and Romansh. Northern Germany is quite low and flat, but in southern Germany the land rises toward the Alps, which cover much of Switzerland and Austria.

The Berlin Wall

After Germany's defeat in World War II (1939–1945), Germany was divided in two, with the eastern part having a Communist government. From 1961 to 1989, a wall split the city of Berlin, separating West Berlin, in West Germany, from East Berlin, in East Germany. The wall was built by East Germany to stop citizens leaving. In 1989, amid great celebrations on both sides, the wall's Brandenburg Gate was opened. In 1990, Germany again became one country.

Although most of the Berlin Wall has been pulled down, some parts remain so people can remember how past troubles have been overcome.

CITY FOCUS: VIENNA

Status: Capital of Austria
Population: 1.9 million
Official language: German
Founded: 1st century
Currency: Euro
Landmark: Schönbrunn Palace, summer home of Austria's kings and queens from 1742 to 1918

Sachertorte, a chocolate cake invented in Vienna

DID YOU KNOW? The Red Cross, an international organization that cares for the sick and wounded in wars and after natural disasters, was founded in Switzerland in 1863.

Nordfriesische Inseln

Deutsche Bucht

Helgoland

Helgoländer Bucht

Ostfriesische Inseln

Bornholm

Kap Arkona

Kieler Bucht

Fehmarn Bælt

Fehmarn

Mecklenburger Bucht

Rügen

Pommersche Bucht

Usedom

Zalew Szczeciński

Hamburg

Bremen

Elbe

Weser

Hannover

Szczecin

Oder

Odra

BERLIN

Warta

Bielefeld

Münster

Uisburg Gelsenkirchen

Esseri Dortmund

Bochum

Wuppertal

Düsseldorf

chen

Cologne

Bonn

Fulda

G E R M A N Y

Elbe

Leipzig

Dresden

Erzgebirge

Germany's factories make more cars than any other European country.

Eifel

Mosel

Wiesbaden

Frankfurt am Main

MBOURG

Mannheim

Karlsruhe

Rhein

Saar

Strasbourg

Vosges

Stuttgart

Schwarzwald

Augsburg

Dona

Nuremberg

Böhmerwald

Donau

Munich

Donau

VIENNA

Neuschwanstein Castle was built for King Ludwig II of Bavaria, now part of Germany, in 1886.

a

Bodensee

Zürich

VADUZ

BERN

LIECHTENSTEIN

S W I T Z E R L A N D

A U S T R I A

Graz

H U N G A R Y

Duna

Drava

The alphorn has no valves or flaps, so the player changes the note using their lips and breath.

Torino

Alphorns

In the Alps, long wooden horns, known as alphorns, were used for communication for hundreds of years. Around 3.5 m (11.5 ft) long, the horns could be heard across mountain valleys. Today, alphorns are used only as musical instruments.

Italy

Italy covers the Italian Peninsula, with its northern border running through the Alps. As well as its largest islands, Sicily and Sardinia, Italy has around 350 smaller islands in the Mediterranean Sea. Since the days of the Roman Empire, Italy has been at the heart of European culture. Today, it has many successful industries, making high-quality cars, clothes, food, and wine.

In Venice, people celebrate Carnival by wearing masks and dressing up.

The Roman Empire

At the start of the 5th century BCE, Rome was a small but fierce city in the middle of the Italian Peninsula. Over the next centuries, the Roman government and army were so well organized that they managed to conquer land far beyond the city walls. By the 3rd century BCE, the Romans had conquered the whole Italian Peninsula. By 117 CE, they ruled Europe from Britain to Greece, plus parts of North Africa and the Middle East. Wherever they ruled, the Romans built cities and roads, as well as introducing their Latin language, laws, and gods.

Completed in 80 CE, Rome's Colosseum was built for holding gladiator fights and other violent shows.

CITY FOCUS: ROME

Status: Capital of Italy

Population: 3.8 million

Official language: Italian

Founded: Around 753 BCE

Currency: Euro

Landmark: The Pantheon, a temple built in 113–25 CE and now used as a church

The Pantheon

106

The Renaissance

The Renaissance (meaning "rebirth") was a time of huge creativity that began in Italian cities in the 14th century. Artists, writers, and architects started to take ideas from the ancient Romans and Greeks, but added their own new ideas about humans, nature, and the universe. The Renaissance spread across Europe.

In 1436, Filippo Brunelleschi's dome for Florence's cathedral changed what people thought was possible to build.

Around 3,326 m (10,912 ft) high, Mount Etna is Italy's largest active volcano and erupts frequently.

SWITZERLAND

LIECHTENSTEIN

Turin
Milan
Verona
Trieste
Venice
Gulf of Venice
Genoa
Golfo di Genova
Bologna
MONACO
Nice **MONACO**
Côte d'Azur
Ligurian Sea
Isola di Gorgona
Cap Corse
Golfo de St-Florent
Isola di Capraia
Corsica
SAN MARINO
Florence
SAN MARINO
Isola d'Elba
Isola Pianosa
Isola di Montecristo
Isola del Giglio
I T A L Y
Kornat
Žirje
Svetac
Strait of Bonifacio
Isola Asinara
Golfo dell' Asinara
VATICAN CITY
ROME
Pianosa
Isole Tremiti
Golfo di Manfredonia
Adriatic Sea
Golfo di Orosei
Golfo di Gaeta
Isola di Ponza
Naples
Bari
Isola d'Ischia
Golfo di Cagliari
Capo Spartivento
Isola di Capri
Golfo di Salerno
Capo Palinuro
Golfo di Policastro
Golfo di Taranto
Othonoi
Capo Santa Maria di Leuca
Kerkyra
Capo San Vito
Isola di Levanzo
Isola Marettimo
Isola Favignana
Palermo
Isola Stromboli
Isola Filicudi
Isola Panarea
Isola Alicudi
Isola Salina
Isola Lipari
Isola Vulcano
Golfo di Squillace
Canale di Sicilia
Mte Etna
Capo Spartivento
Catania
Stretto di Messina
Sicily
Ionian Sea
Isola di Pantelleria
Canale di Malta
Capo Passero

DID YOU KNOW? Two microstates are completely surrounded by Italy: San Marino and Vatican City, which is home to the head of the Catholic Church, the Pope.

Greece

Greece lies on the southern Balkan Peninsula. Around 6,000 islands, large and small, are also scattered in the Aegean and Ionian Seas, which are parts of the Mediterranean Sea. The largest island is Crete, which was the site of Europe's first civilization, the Minoan, which lasted from around 2700 BCE to 1100 BCE.

The island of Corfu is said to have up to 4 million olive trees.

Ancient Greece

From the 8th century BCE, the cities of Greece grew powerful. Each city, such as Athens, Sparta, and Corinth, controlled the surrounding land. The cities were home to great thinkers, architects, and artists. They came up with new ideas about the stars, mathematics, and science. Elegant new public buildings were constructed. There were temples for the 12 major gods and goddesses, including Zeus and Hera, as well as many minor ones.

Delphi, in central Greece, was a religious site for people from all the Greek cities. This round temple was built for the goddess Athena in around 360 BCE. Athena was goddess of wisdom, war, and the important city of Athens.

From around 776 BCE to 393 CE, sportspeople from all Greek cities competed at the Olympic Games, held in Olympia every four years.

CITY FOCUS: ATHENS

Status: Capital of Greece
Population: 3 million
Official language: Greek
Founded: Around 3000 BCE
Currency: Euro
Landmark: The Parthenon, a temple to the goddess Athena completed in 432 BCE

The Parthenon

DONIA

Gotse Delchev
Smolyan
Kürdzhali
Edirne
Sariyer

Gevgelija
Paranestio
Orestiada
Uzunköprü
İstanbul

Polykastro
Sidirokastro
Xanthi
Komotini
Hayrabolu
Muratlı
Silivri

Serres
Souli
Keşan

Kilkis
Drama
Alexandroupoli

Edessa
Nea Zichni
Eleftheroupoli
Kavala

Naousa
Platy
Thasos
Thasos
Thrakiko Pelagos

ida
Poligiros
Theologos
Saros Körfezi

Veroia
Kolpos
Orfanou
Kolpos Ierissou
Ierissos
Samothraki

ni
Katerini
Epanomi
Karyes
Samothraki

Servia
Thessaloniki
Ákra Pinnes
Gökçeada

Olympos △
2911m
Thermaïkos
Kolpos
Sikea
Limnos

Elassona
Kolpos Agiou Orous
Moudros
Çanakkale Boğazı

Tyrnavos
Larisa
Myrina
Bozcaada

kala
Agios
Efstratios

a
G R E E C E
Gioura
Mithymna

Sofades
Volos
Kyra Panagia
Sporades
Lesvos
Mytilini

Almyros
Milies
Skiathos
Plomari

Pagasitikos
Kolpos
Alonnisos

Stylida
Skopelos
Skyros

Lamia
Istiaia
Mantoudi
Skyros

nisi
Limni
Kym

Lidoriki
Voreios Evvoïkos Kolpos
Psara
Kardamila

gi
Atalanti
Chios
Chios

Chalkida
Levadia
Evvoia
Chios

Antikyra
Thiva
Aegean

Aigio
Acharnes
Marathonas
Neo Karlovasi
Kuşadası i Körfezi

Gulf of Corinth
Megara
Karystos
Andros
Sea
Samos

ryta
Xylokastro
Piraeus
ATHENS
Ándros
Ikaria
Agios Kirykos

Dafni
Korinthos
Salamina
Lavrio
Tinos
Ikaria

Argos
Aigina
Kea
Mykonos

Tripoli
Nafplio
Methana
Ke
Patmos
Güllük
Körfezi

Megalopoli
Ermioni
Kythnos
Syros
Leros
Kalymnos

Argolikos Kolpos
Ydra
Ermoupoli
Dodecanese
Kalymnos
Kos

Spetses
Cyclades
Naxos
Kefalos

Kalamata
Serifos
Paros
Amorgos
Kos

Mirtoö
Pelagos
Sifnos
Irakleia
Symi

Gytheio
Sykea
Milos
Sikinos
Ios
Nisyros
Tilos
Rhodes

Areopoli
Neapoli
Milos
Ios
Anafi
Astypalaia
Kalavarda
Fethiye
Körfezi

Lakonikos
Kolpos
Folegandros
Chalki

kra Tainaro
Thira
Monolithos
Lindos
Megisti

Kythira
Kythira
Kattavia
Rhodes

Saria

Antikythira
Kolpos
Chanion
Crete
Olympos
Karpathos

Kastelli
Chania
Karpathos

Heraklion
Akra
Sideros
Kasos

Rethymno
Skopi

Palaiochora
Agios Nikolaos
Siteia

Tympaki
Ierapetra

Gavdos

Rocky Hideouts

At Meteora, near Trikala in central Greece, rock pillars were left standing after the surrounding rock was worn away. From the 14th century, Christian monks built monasteries on the pillars so they could pray quietly and escape raids by the Turks.

When they were first built, the monasteries at Meteora could be reached only by ladder or rope.

DID YOU KNOW? In 508–507 BCE, Athens was the first place to introduce democracy, a system of government in which people get a say on how their country is run by casting votes.

The Balkans

The Balkan Peninsula takes its name from the Balkan Mountains, which stretch across Bulgaria from the border with Serbia to the Black Sea. This is a region of many different peoples, languages, and religions, including Eastern Orthodox Christianity, Catholic Christianity, and Islam.

Lipizzaner Horses

Lipizzaner horses are a breed that was developed in the 16th century in Lipica, in modern Slovenia. Lipizzaners are muscly, long-lived, and usually have a white coat. In Lipica, as well as in the Spanish Riding School in Austria, the horses are trained for dressage. In dressage, horses and riders perform careful movements, balances, and jumps, often to music.

Today, Romania is a democracy and the Palace of Parliament is home to the country's lawmakers.

A Lipizzaner performs a pesade by standing on its hind legs.

World's Heaviest Building

The Palace of Parliament in Bucharest, Romania, weighs around 4 billion kg (8.8 billion lb). It was built for Nicolae Ceauşescu, who ruled Romania as a dictator, holding complete power from 1965 to 1989.

From the 12th century, the walled city of Dubrovnik, in Croatia, became a wealthy trading port.

DID YOU KNOW? From 1918 to 1992, Slovenia, Croatia, Bosnia and Herzegovina, Serbia, Montenegro, Kosovo, and North Macedonia were united as one country: Yugoslavia.

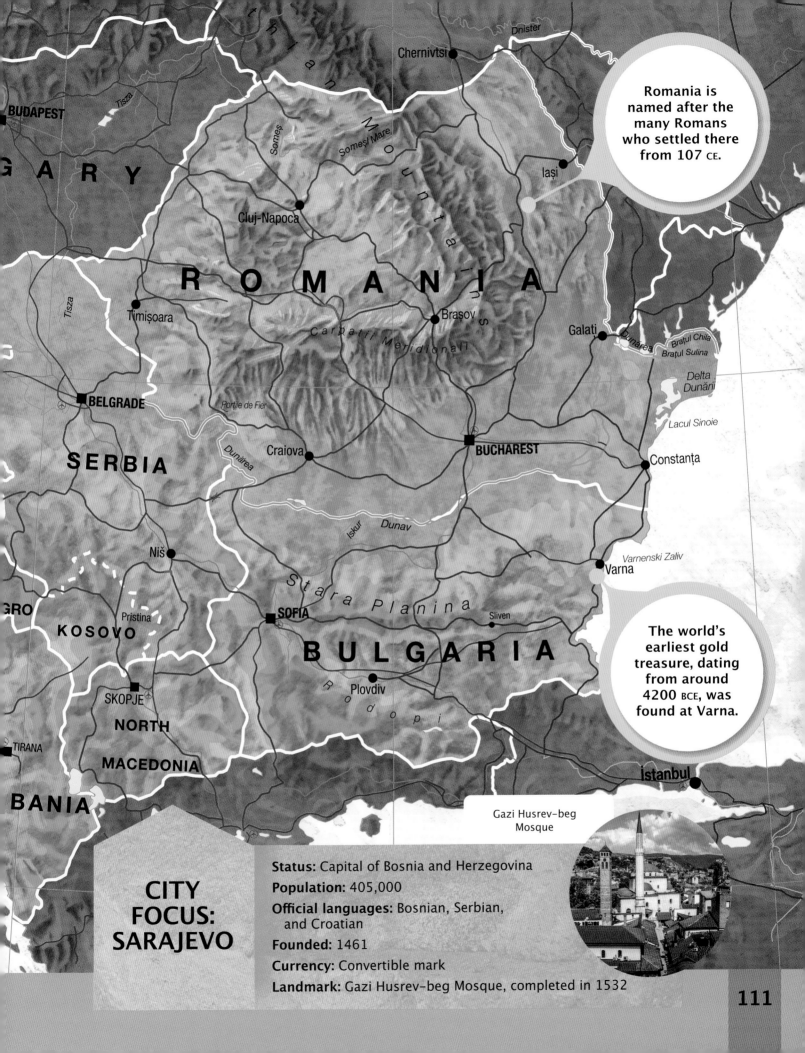

Romania is named after the many Romans who settled there from 107 CE.

The world's earliest gold treasure, dating from around 4200 BCE, was found at Varna.

CITY FOCUS: SARAJEVO

Status: Capital of Bosnia and Herzegovina

Population: 405,000

Official languages: Bosnian, Serbian, and Croatian

Founded: 1461

Currency: Convertible mark

Landmark: Gazi Husrev-beg Mosque, completed in 1532

Gazi Husrev-beg Mosque

Eastern Europe

From 1947 to 1989, the countries of Eastern Europe had Communist governments. Today, they have moved toward capitalism, a system in which most trade and industry are owned by individuals. Despite these similarities, the countries of this region are proud of their own languages, histories, and traditions, from the fishing festivals of Estonia to the violinists of Hungary. The landscape ranges from wide forests and farmland to large, industrial cities.

Flower Cottages

The villagers of Zalipie, in Poland, have a tradition of painting their wooden cottages with flower patterns. The tradition was begun by the women of the village, who made their own brushes from the tails of their cows.

Zalipie is famous for keeping its traditions alive.

Széchenyi, in Budapest, is the largest thermal bath complex in Europe.

Thermal Baths

In Hungary, there are many thermal springs where the water has been heated inside the Earth. The Romans were the first to build public baths over these springs. Many more baths were built when Hungary was ruled by the Turks, who also enjoyed relaxing in hot water. From the 19th century, grand bath complexes were opened where people could exercise, rest, chat, and eat.

ESTONIA

Hiiumaa
aremaa

TALLINN

Gulf of Riga

RIGA **LATVIA**

Daugava

LITHUANIA

Nemunas
SIA
Kaunas

VILNIUS

Hrodna

Neman

B E L A R U S

ND
Bug
AW
Brest

Lublin

Prypyats'

Dnyapro

Vitsyebsk

MINSK   Mahilyow

Homyel'

Chernihiv

L'viv

Rivne

Zhytomyr

KIEV

Khmel'nyts'kyy   Vinnytsya

U K R A I N E

Chernivtsi

Dnister

Oleksandriya

Cherkasy

Poltava

Sumy

Kursk

Belgorod

Kharkiv

Luhans'k

Horlivka
Donets'k Makiyivka
Dnipropetrovs'k

Kryvyy Rih   Zaporizhzhya

Taganrog

Rostov-na-Donu

Mariupol'

MOLDOVA

Iaşi   CHIŞINĂU

Prut

Mykolayiv

Dnipro
Kherson

Odesa

Sea of Azov

Galaţi Dunărea Bratul Chila
Bratul Sulina

Dnister

Crimean
Peninsula

Kuban

Laba
Krasnodar

Simferopol'

Novorossiysk

Sevastopol'

CITY FOCUS: TALLINN

Status: Capital of Estonia
Population: 435,000
Official language: Estonian
Founded: 10th century
Currency: Euro
Landmark: The City Wall, begun in 1265

Tallinn

The Kiev Monastery of the Caves was founded in 1051 when one Eastern Orthdox Christian monk, Anthony, moved into a cave here.

Ukraine is one of the world's largest growers of grain crops, such as wheat, maize, and barley.

The national sport of Moldova is *trântă*, a type of wrestling.

DID YOU KNOW? The Czech Republic is one of the least religious countries in the world, with around three-quarters of its people saying that they do not believe in any religion.

113

Oceania

The region of Oceania includes the continent of Australia, the islands of New Zealand, and three Pacific Ocean island groups. These are Melanesia, stretching from Papua New Guinea in the west to Fiji in the east; Micronesia, to the north, ranging from Palau to Kiribati; and Polynesia, covering the islands east and north of Tonga.

The Ring of Fire

The Ring of Fire is a roughly arch-shaped band around the edges of the Pacific Ocean. This band is the site of 75 percent of the world's volcanoes, as well as 90 percent of all earthquakes. This activity is caused by the movement of the tectonic plates that lie underneath the Pacific Ocean.

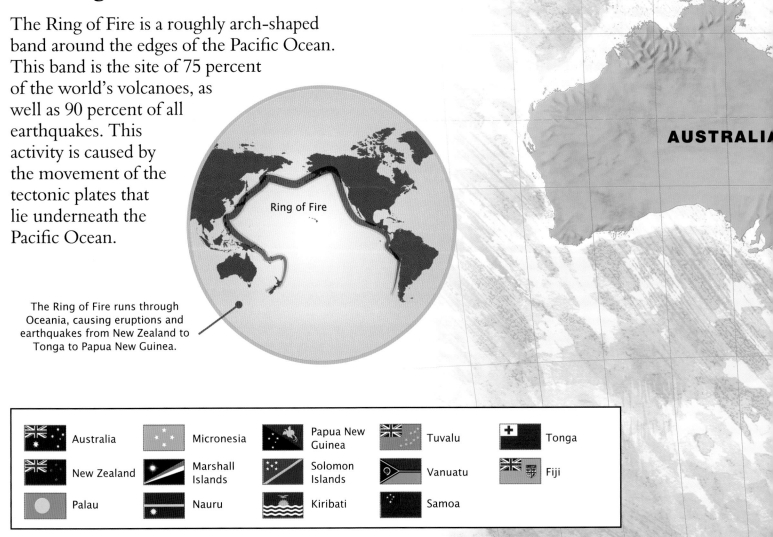

Ring of Fire

The Ring of Fire runs through Oceania, causing eruptions and earthquakes from New Zealand to Tonga to Papua New Guinea.

PALAU

AUSTRALIA

Australia	Micronesia	Papua New Guinea	Tuvalu	Tonga
New Zealand	Marshall Islands	Solomon Islands	Vanuatu	Fiji
Palau	Nauru	Kiribati	Samoa	

DID YOU KNOW? Australia is the country in Oceania with the largest population, 26 million people, while Tuvalu has the smallest, with around 11,000 people.

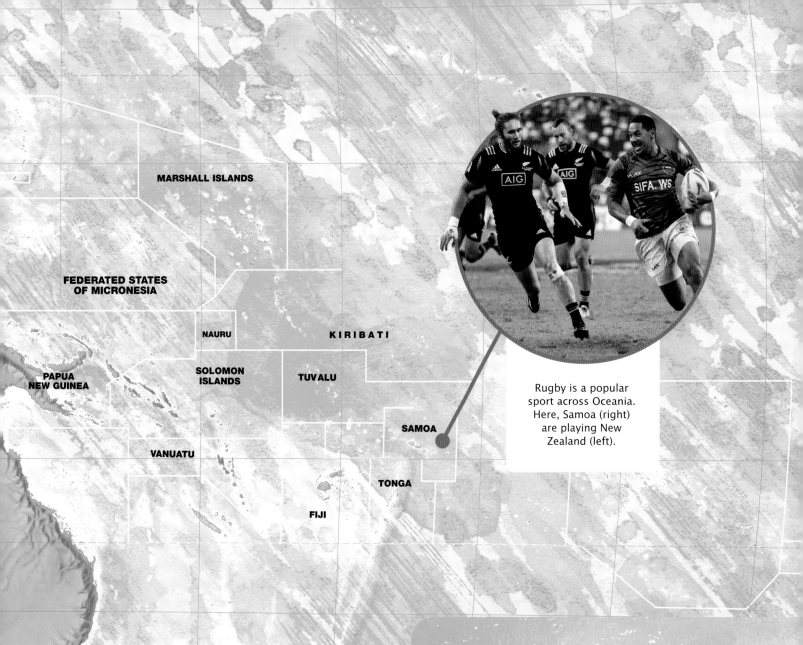

MARSHALL ISLANDS

FEDERATED STATES
OF MICRONESIA

NAURU

KIRIBATI

PAPUA
NEW GUINEA

SOLOMON
ISLANDS

TUVALU

SAMOA

VANUATU

TONGA

FIJI

NEW ZEALAND

Rugby is a popular
sport across Oceania.
Here, Samoa (right)
are playing New
Zealand (left).

Canoe Exploration

The first people to live in Melanesia,
Micronesia, Polynesia, and New Zealand
arrived by canoe. In around 1500 BCE, the
earliest groups set sail from Asia, settling
on the western islands. Over thousands of
years, people moved farther and
farther to the east, northeast, and
southeast, finally reaching New
Zealand around 1200 CE.

Craftspeople still build wooden canoes
using traditional methods, with an
outrigger, or float, for balance.

Australia

Aboriginal Australians and Torres Strait Islanders had been living in Australia for around 50,000 years before the first European settlers arrived, in 1788. Today, the majority of Australians live around the continent's coasts, particularly in the southeast. Much of the interior is desert or scrubby dry land, known as the outback.

More than 1,500 species of fish live on the reef.

The Great Barrier Reef

The Great Barrier Reef is the world's largest coral reef system, made up of over 2,900 individual reefs. It stretches for 2,300 km (1,400 miles) off the east coast of northeastern Australia. Reefs are rocky ridges made of the skeletons of millions of tiny animals called coral polyps. Like all reefs, the Great Barrier Reef is at risk from rising sea temperatures and pollution.

Uluru

In central Australia is a vast block of sandstone, known as Uluru. It is 348 m (1,142 ft) high and 9.4 km (5.8 miles) around. While the surrounding softer rock was worn away over millions of years, the sandstone remained.

Uluru is sacred to the Anangu Aboriginal people.

Parliament House

CITY FOCUS: CANBERRA

Status: Capital of Australia
Population: 420,000
Official language: English
Founded: 1913
Currency: Australian dollar
Landmark: Parliament House, built in 1988 and topped by an 81-m (266-ft) flagpole

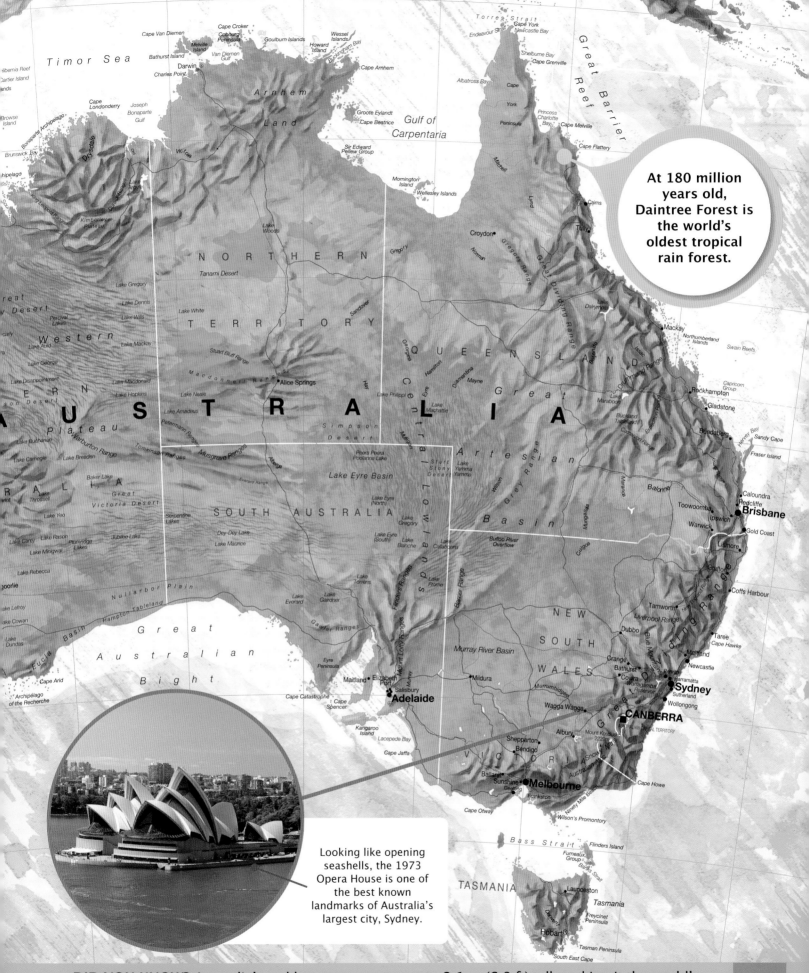

Timor Sea

Cape Van Diemen
Cape Croker
Coburg
Peninsula
Melville
Island
Bathurst Island?
Van Diemen
Gulf
Charles Point
Darwin

Goulburn Islands
Howard
Island
Buckingham Bay
Cape Arnhem

Arnhem
Land

Wessel
Islands

Torres Strait
Cape York
Newcastle Bay
Endeavour Strait
Shelburne Bay
Cape Grenville

Albatross Bay
Cape
York
Princess Charlotte
Bay
Cape Melville

Cape Flattery

Great Barrier Reef

Groote Eylandt
Cape Beatrice

Gulf of
Carpentaria

Sir Edward
Pellew Group

Mornington
Island
Wellesley Islands

Cairns
Tully
Croydon
Noman
Gregory

NORTHERN

TERRITORY

Tanami Desert

Lake
Woods

Lake Dalrymple
Mackay
Northumberland
Islands
Swain Reefs

Lake Gregory
Lake Dennis
Lake Wills
Lake White
Sandover

Percival
Lakes
Western
Lake Arid
Lake Mackay
Stuart Bluff Range

Macdonnell Ranges
Alice Springs

QUEENSLAND
Hamilton
Mayne

Great

Rockhampton
Capricorn
Group
Gladstone

Lake Macdonald
Lake Hopkins
Lake Neale
Lake Amadeus
Petermann Ranges

Simpson
Desert

Diamantina

Bundaberg
Hervey Bay
Sandy Cape
Fraser Island

AUSTRALIA

Musgrave Ranges
Tomkinson Ranges

Peera Peera
Poolanna Lake

Artesian
Grey Range

Caloundra
Redcliffe
Brisbane
Ipswich
Gold Coast

Everard Range

Lake Eyre Basin

Stuart
Stony
Desert

Basin

Toowoomba
Warwick

Lismore

Victoria Desert

SOUTH AUSTRALIA

Lake Eyre
(North)

Lake
Gregory
Lake Eyre
(South)
Lake
Blanche
Lake Callabonna

Buffalo River
Overflow

Grafton
Coffs Harbour

Serpentine
Lakes
Dey-Dey Lake
Lake Maurice

Flinders Ranges

Lake Frome

Tamworth
Liverpool Range

Taree
Cape Hawke

Nullarbor Plain
Hampton Tableland

Lake
Torrens
Lake Everard
Lake Gairdner

Barrier Range

Dubbo

NEW
SOUTH
WALES

Maitland
Newcastle

Great
Australian
Bight

Gawler Ranges

Eyre
Peninsula

Mount Lofty Ranges

Murray River Basin

Mildura
Murrumbidgee
Wagga Wagga

Orange
Bathurst
Cowra

Blue Mountains
Warragamba
Reservoir

Parramatta
Sydney
Sutherland
Wollongong

Maitland
Elizabeth
Port
Salisbury
Adelaide

Cape Catastrophe
Cape
Spencer

Kangaroo
Island
Lacepede Bay

CANBERRA

Shepparton
Bendigo
Albury
Mount Kosciuszko
2228m

VICTORIA
Snowy
Australian Alps

Ballarat
Sunshine
Melbourne
Geelong
Frankston

Cape Howe

Cape Jaffa

Cape Otway

Ninety Mile Beach

Wilson's Promontory

Bass Strait
Flinders Island

Furneaux
Group
Banks Strait

TASMANIA
Launceston
Tasmania
Freycinet
Peninsula

Hobart
Tasman Peninsula
South East Cape

At 180 million years old, Daintree Forest is the world's oldest tropical rain forest.

Looking like opening seashells, the 1973 Opera House is one of the best known landmarks of Australia's largest city, Sydney.

DID YOU KNOW? Australia's red kangaroo grows up to 2.1 m (6.9 ft) tall, making it the world's largest marsupial, a group of mammals known for carrying their young in a pouch.

New Zealand

New Zealand lies on two main islands, North Island and South Island, and around 600 smaller ones. New Zealand's first settlers, called the Maori, brought with them their eastern Polynesian language and traditions. Europeans, mostly from the British Isles, started to settle from the start of the 19th century.

Geysers

Due to its location on the Ring of Fire, New Zealand has frequent earthquakes and volcanic eruptions. North Island is home to several geysers. Geysers are found where water soaks into the ground and is heated by magma. The water boils, its pressure rising, resulting in hot water and steam spraying out of a crack in the ground at regular intervals.

Pohutu Geyser spurts up to 30 m (100 ft) around 20 times a day. (Pohutu means "Big Splash" in Maori.)

The Haka

The haka is a Maori dance performed by men or women, who stamp their feet and chant. In the past, war haka were used to frighten the enemy before battle, with warriors grimacing, sticking out their tongues, and waving weapons. Today, the haka is perfomed as a celebration.

Maori dancers perform for a national holiday.

Steep Mitre Peak rises above Milford Sound, a fjord carved by glaciers over millions of years.

Milford S

Lake Ana

Resolution Island   Manap

Cape Providence   Ora

Fo

Stewart Island
Southwest Cape

DID YOU KNOW? New Zealand was part of the British Empire from 1841 to 1947, when the country gained full independence from the United Kingdom.

Three Kings Islands

North Cape
Cape Reinga
Te Kao
Great Exhibition Bay
Ninety Mile Beach
Awanui
Kaitaia
Okaihau
Russell
Kawakawa
Cape Brett
Whangarei
Dargaville
Walotira
Paparoa
Kaipara Harbour
Great Barrier Island
East Coast Bays
Helensville
Hauraki Gulf
Port Jackson
Takapuna
Auckland
Coromandel Peninsula
Manukau
Thames
Waihi

North Island
(Te Ika-a-Māui)

Paeroa
Bay of Plenty
Cape Runaway
Te Araroa
Tauranga
Matata
Whakatane
East Cape
Hamilton
Te Awamutu
Putaruru
Kawerau
Opotiki
Albatross Point
Tokoroa
Rotorua
Murupara
Lake Taupo
North Taranaki Bight
Awakino
Taumarunui
Taupo
Gisborne
Wairoa
New Plymouth
Waitara
Mahia Peninsula
Cape Egmont
Stratford
Hawke Bay
Eltham
Napier
Hawera
Taihape
Cape Kidnappers
Hunterville
Hastings
Wanganui
Marton
Dannevirke
South Taranaki Basin
Palmerston North
Cape Farewell
D'Urville Island
Levin
Masterton
Castlepoint
Collingwood
Tasman Bay
Porirua
Karamea Bight
Nelson
Picton
Upper Hutt
Lower Hutt
Richmond
WELLINGTON
Westport
Blenheim
Cape Palliser
Seddon
Ward
Cape Campbell

South Island
(Te Waipounamu)

Reefton
Kaikoura
Greymouth
Waiau
Hokitika
Cheviot
Waipara
Pegasus Bay
Harihari
Kaiapoi
Aoraki
Christchurch
Aoraki (Mount Cook) 3724m
Lyttelton
Banks Peninsula
Akaroa
Head
Mount
spiring
030m
Canterbury Bight
Timaru
Southern Alps
Waimate
Lake Wanaka
Omarama
Oamaru
Queenstown
Hampden
Lake akatipu
Alexandra
Waikouaiti
Palmerston
Roxburgh
Port Chalmers
Lumsden
Dunedin
Gore
Winton
Invercargill
Balclutha
Bluff
Halfmoon Bay

Pegasus

NEW ZEALAND

A bungee jumper, tied to an elastic rope, dangles from Auckland's 328-m (1,076-ft) Sky Tower, the tallest structure south of the equator.

North Island's highest mountain is the volcano Mount Ruapehu, 2,797 m (9,177 ft) tall.

Chatham Islands (New Zealand)
Point Somes
Chatham Island
Petrie Bay
Pitt Island

CITY FOCUS: WELLINGTON

Status: Capital of New Zealand

Population: 418,000

Official languages: English, Maori, and New Zealand Sign Language

Founded: From the 13th century

Currency: New Zealand dollar

Landmark: Wellington Cable Car

Wellington Cable Car

Bounty Islands (New Zealand)

Pacific Ocean

The world's largest ocean covers one-third of Earth's surface, 165 million sq km (63.8 million sq miles). The Pacific is also the deepest ocean, reaching a depth of 10,984 m (36,037 ft) in the Mariana Trench, close to the Mariana Islands.

Rising Sea Levels

The oceans are rising because of an increase in worldwide temperatures. When ocean water warms up, it expands. In addition, ice is melting in polar regions, adding water to the oceans. During the 21st century, the oceans are predicted to rise by 30–130 cm (1–4.3 ft), putting low islands and coasts at risk. A key cause of rising temperatures is the burning of fossil fuels, such as coal and oil, which releases carbon dioxide. This gas traps the Sun's heat in Earth's atmosphere.

The Marshall Islands are among the many island countries threatened by rising sea levels.

CITY FOCUS: TARAWA

Status: Capital of Kiribati

Population: 56,000

Official languages: English and Gilbertese

Founded: From the 1st century

Currencies: Kiribati and Australian dollars

Landmark: The House of Assembly, meetingplace of the country's lawmakers

House of Assembly

SEA OF OKHOTSK

NORTH KOREA

SEA OF JAPAN (EAST SEA)

JAPAN

SOUTH KOREA

(YELLOW SEA)

EAST CHINA SEA

TAIWAN

PHILIPPINE SEA

SOUTH CHINA SEA

PHILIPPINES

NORTHERN MARIANA ISLANDS (U.S.A.)

MICRON

SULU SEA

BRUNEI

SABAH

MALAYSIA

SARAWAK

CELEBES SEA

PALAU

FEDERATED STATES OF MICRONESIA

INDONESIA

Pegunungan Maoke

Bismarck Archipelago

MELA

FLORES SEA

BANDA SEA

EAST TIMOR

ARAFURA SEA

Torres Strait

PAPUA NEW GUINEA

Joseph Bonaparte Gulf

Arnhem Land

Gulf of Carpentaria

CORAL SEA

CORAL SEA ISLANDS TERRITORY (Austr.)

TIMOR SEA

Kimberley Plateau

NORTHERN

TERRITORY

GREAT SANDY DESERT

QUEENSLAND

WESTERN

GIBSON DESERT

AUSTRALIA

AUSTRALIA

GREAT VICTORIA DESERT

SOUTH AUSTRALIA

GREAT DIVIDING RANGE

Nullarbor Plain

NEW SOUTH WALES

Great Australian Bight

VICTORIA

Bass Strait

TASMAN SEA

TASMANIA

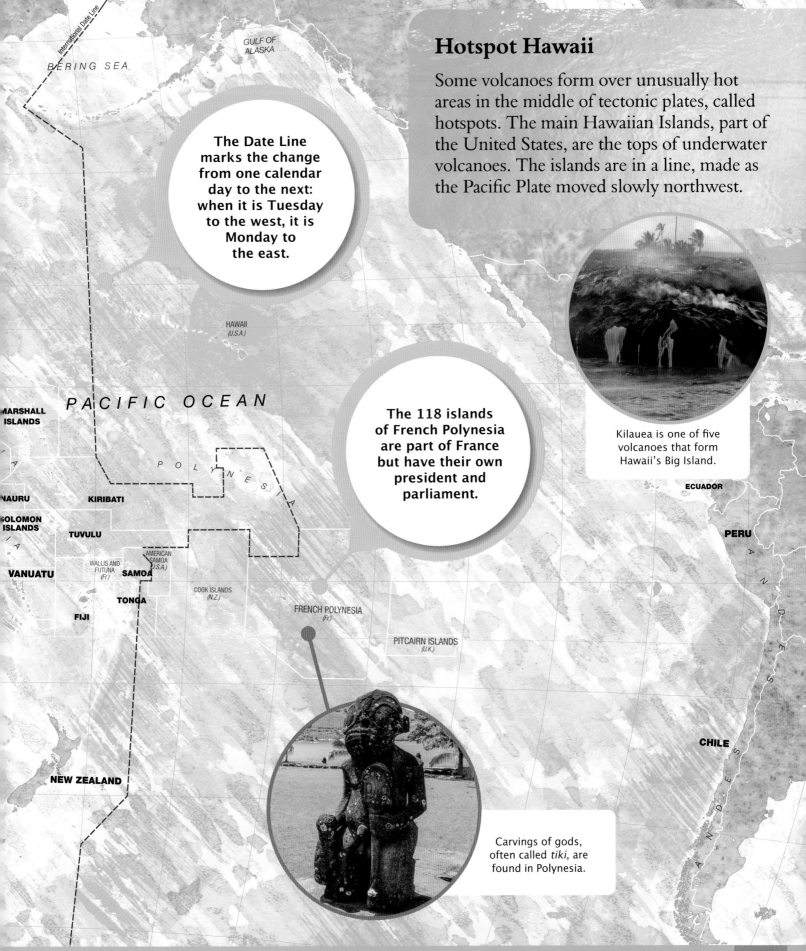

Hotspot Hawaii

Some volcanoes form over unusually hot areas in the middle of tectonic plates, called hotspots. The main Hawaiian Islands, part of the United States, are the tops of underwater volcanoes. The islands are in a line, made as the Pacific Plate moved slowly northwest.

The Date Line marks the change from one calendar day to the next: when it is Tuesday to the west, it is Monday to the east.

The 118 islands of French Polynesia are part of France but have their own president and parliament.

Kilauea is one of five volcanoes that form Hawaii's Big Island.

Carvings of gods, often called *tiki*, are found in Polynesia.

International Date Line

BERING SEA

GULF OF ALASKA

HAWAII (U.S.A.)

PACIFIC OCEAN

POLYNESIA

MARSHALL ISLANDS

NAURU

KIRIBATI

SOLOMON ISLANDS

TUVULU

VANUATU

WALLIS AND FUTUNA (Fr.)

AMERICAN SAMOA (U.S.A.)

SAMOA

FIJI

TONGA

COOK ISLANDS (N.Z.)

FRENCH POLYNESIA (Fr.)

PITCAIRN ISLANDS (U.K.)

ECUADOR

PERU

CHILE

ANDES

NEW ZEALAND

DID YOU KNOW? The Pacific Ocean was named Mar Pacífico ("Peaceful Sea") in 1521, by Portuguese explorer Ferdinand Magellan during the first ever voyage round the world.

The Arctic

In winter, the Arctic sea ice stretches to the coast of Alaska.

The Arctic is the region around the North Pole, which lies in the Arctic Ocean. This ocean is always partly covered by ice, while the surrounding land has a layer of frozen ground, called permafrost. Parts of Canada, the United States, Russia, Finland, Sweden, Norway, Iceland, and Greenland are in the Arctic.

The Northern Lights

The Northern Lights are lights in the sky, seen in the Arctic during winter, when the Sun does not appear, or only briefly appears, above the horizon. The lights are caused by particles that stream out from the Sun. These give energy to gases in Earth's atmosphere, which release the energy as light. The lights appear around the North Pole, as well as around the South Pole, because Earth's magnetic field guides the Sun's particles toward the poles.

Different gases create green, pink, and blue lights.

Fairbanks

ALASKA
(U.S.A.)

Barrow

Prudhoe Bay

Ch
Se

Inuvik

Beaufort
Sea

C
A
N
A
D
A

Banks
Island

Victoria
Island

Parry
Islands

Queen Elizabeth
Islands

Ellesmere Island

Nares Strait

Southampton
Island

Foxe
Basin

Thule

M

Merville
Bay

Peary Land

Hudson Strait

Baffin Island

Baffin
Bay

Iqaluit

Upernavik

Davis Strait

GREENLAND
(Den.)

Gunnbjørn Fjeld
▲ 12136ft

Ammassalik

Denmark Strait

Arctic Circ

ATLANTIC
OCEAN

REYKJAVÍK

ICELAND

122

Wrangel
Island

East Siberian
Sea

New Siberian
Islands

Tiksi

Laptev Sea

Taymyr Peninsula

ARCTIC
OCEAN

Severnaya
Zemlya

North Pole

Franz Josefs Land
(Rus.)

Jesup

Kap Zelanya

Kara
Sea

Vorkuta

Nordostrundingen

Nordaustlandet

Novaya
Zemlya

Greenland
Sea

Svalbard
(Nor.)

Barents
Sea

Kolguyev

Bear Island
(Bjørnøya)
(Nor.)

Nordkapp

an Mayen Island
(Nor.)

Tromsø

Murmansk

Norwegian
Sea

NORWAY

SWEDEN

FINLAND

Status: City in Russia and largest city in the Arctic

Population: 307,000

Official language: Russian

Founded: 1916

Currency: Russian rouble

Landmark: Alyosha Monument

CITY FOCUS: MURMANSK

The 35.5-m (116-ft) Alyosha Monument

Traditional Inuit Life

Inuit peoples live in the Arctic regions of the United States, Canada, and Greenland, which is part of Denmark. Today, few Inuit lead traditional lives, but some still hunt whales, muskoxen, and seals. During the winter, some build a shelter from snow, called an igloo. While most Inuit now use snowmobiles to get around, some still make use of dog sleds.

In Greenland, an Inuit fisherman has dug a hole in the ice to catch fish.

Polar bears spend most of their life hunting for seals on the ice that floats on the surface of the Arctic Ocean.

DID YOU KNOW? The Arctic is warmed by the Arctic Ocean, which never falls below −2°C (28°F), so the temperature does not usually fall below −50°C (−58 °F), even at the North Pole.

123

The Antarctic

Earth's southernmost continent, surrounded by the Southern Ocean, is the site of the South Pole. Antarctica is not owned by any country, but up to 4,000 scientists from many countries work there in research stations. Only a few remain through the winter, when the Sun does not rise for 11 weeks.

The northern Antarctic Peninsula is the only part of the continent not covered in ice.

Death on the Ice

During the Antarctic summer of 1911–12, two teams of explorers raced to be the first to reach the South Pole: a British team led by Robert Falcon Scott, and a Norwegian team led by Roald Amundsen. The well-organized Amundsen team won the race, reaching the Pole on 14 December 1911. Scott reached it a month later, finding his rival's flag. On the way back to their base, Scott and his four companions died from hunger and cold.

In 1911, Scott's team built this base at Cape Evans, on the Antarctic coast.

DID YOU KNOW? The Sun never rises high in the sky at the poles, making the interior of Antarctica the coldest place on Earth, with a lowest temperature of −89.2°C (−128.6°F).

SOUTHERN OCEAN

Antarctic Circle

Fimbul Ice Shelf
Jelbart Ice Shelf
Neumayer III (Germany)
SANAE IV (South Africa)
Troll (Norway)
Tor (Norway)
Maitri (India)
Novolazarevskaya (Russia)
Princess Elisabeth (Belgium)
Asuka (Japan)
Syowa (Japan)
Jinnah (Pakistan)
Kohnen (Germany)
Dome Fuji (Japan)

East Antarctica

Valkyrie Dome

Wilma Glacier

N. Maitri (Russia)

Cape Darnley

Amery Ice Shelf

Progress (Russia)
Davis (Australia)
Zhongshan (China)
Bharati (India)

Taishan (China)

Kunlun (China)

South Polar Plateau

Amundsen-Scott (U.S.A.)
South Pole
Nico

South Geomagnetic Pole (2015)

Vostok (Russia)

Concordia (France/Italy)

Antarctic Mountains

Brandberg
Mt. Simtel Glacier
Byrd Glacier
Britannia Range

Ross Ice Shelf

Roosevelt Island

Scott Base (N.Z.)
McMurdo (U.S.A.)
Marble Point
Ross Island

ROSS SEA

Mario Zucchelli (Italy)
Jang Bogo (Rep. of Korea)
Cape Washington

Mariner Glacier

Cape Adare

Cape Cheetham

Mertz Glacier

Oates Land

Dumont d'Urville (France)

HJ115

Antarctica is the highest continent, with an average height of 2,500 m (8,200 ft).

Penguins

Very few animals can survive on Antarctica, but a few seals and birds visit the coasts. Adélie, chinstrap, emperor, gentoo, and macaroni penguins spend part of their year on Antarctica. Unable to fly, penguins dive in the ocean to catch fish and squid. They come ashore to lay eggs and care for their chicks.

Adélie penguins mate on the Antarctic coast in summer, from October to February.

Flags of 12 countries stand near the geographic South Pole, the southern point on Earth's surface that crosses its axis of rotation.

McMurdo Station

CITY FOCUS: McMURDO STATION

Status: United States research station and largest settlement in Antarctica

Population: 1,258 summer, 250 winter

Official language: English

Founded: 1956

Currency: United States dollar

Landmark: The bright blue café and shop

Glossary

AXIS OF ROTATION
The line joining the North and South Poles, around which Earth rotates daily.

BIODIVERSITY
The variety of animals and plants in an area or in the world.

BIOME
An area where a particular group of animals and plants live, all suited to the climate and other conditions.

BUDDHISM
A religion based on the teachings of Siddhartha Guatama, the Buddha, who lived in India between the 6th and 4th centuries BCE.

CANAL
A narrow human-made waterway designed to enable boats and ships to travel inland.

CANYON
A narrow valley, usually worn away by a river over thousands of years.

CAPITAL
The city or town that is the meeting place of a country or state's government.

CHRISTIANITY
A religion based on the teachings of Jesus Christ, including the Catholic, Protestant, and Eastern Orthodox Churches.

CIVILIZATION
An ordered society, usually based around cities, where people perform different jobs, such as leaders, craftspeople, and priests.

CLIMATE
The usual weather in a region, year after year.

COMMUNISM
A system of government in which all property, such as businesses, is owned by the community.

CONDENSE
To change from a gas into a liquid.

CONIFEROUS FOREST
An area with many trees that have needle-shaped or scale-like leaves, which usually do not fall from the tree before winter.

CONTINENT
A large land mass, usually surrounded by water and containing many different countries.

COUNTRY
An area of land that has its own government.

CURRENCY
The money used by a particular country or group of countries.

DECIDUOUS FOREST
An area with many trees that have broad, flat leaves, which fall from the tree at a particular time of year.

DEMOCRACY
A system of government in which the people get a say in law-making, usually by voting for their representatives in a parliament.

DENSITY
The number of people or things in a place, compared with its size.

DESERT
An area that gets less than 25 cm (10 in) of rain per year.

DICTATOR
A ruler who has not been elected by the people and holds total power.

DYNASTY
A series of rulers who are all from the same family.

EARTHQUAKE
A shaking of the ground, caused by movements of Earth's tectonic plates.

EMPIRE
A group of countries or regions that are governed by one ruler or country.

ENDANGERED
At risk of dying out.

EQUATOR
An imaginary line around Earth's middle, dividing it into northern and southern halves.

EVAPORATE
To change from a liquid into a gas.

EXECUTIVE CAPITAL
In countries with more than one capital city, the city where the government offices are based.

FJORD
A narrow valley carved by ice and flooded by the sea.

GOVERNMENT
A group of people who are responsible for a country or state.

HEAD OF STATE
The person who represents a country in public, such as a president, king, or queen.

HINDUISM
A religion that grew in India after 500 BCE, with a belief in one God who takes many forms that are recognized as different gods.

HOT SPRING
Water that rises to Earth's surface after being heated underground.

HUMID
When the air is very damp.

ICE AGE
A period when Earth was much colder than today and large regions were covered by ice.

INDIGENOUS PEOPLES
Groups of people whose ancestors were early inhabitants of a region.

ISLAM
A religion based on the teachings of the Prophet Muhammad, who was born in Mecca, in modern Saudi Arabia, in around 570 CE.

ISTHMUS
A narrow strip of land that links two larger areas of land.

JUDAISM
A religion that developed in the region of modern Israel from around 2000 BCE.

LANDLOCKED
Surrounded by land, with no access to the sea.

LAVA
Rock that has melted underground, then erupted from a volcano.

LEGISLATIVE CAPITAL
In countries with more than one capital city, the city where the people's elected representatives meet to discuss new laws.

MAGMA
Rock that has melted inside Earth.

MAMMAL
An animal with hair or fur; female mammals feed their babies on milk.

MICROSTATE
A very small country.

NATIONAL LANGUAGE
A language spoken by most of a country's people.

NATURAL RESOURCE
Materials found in nature, such as wood and metals, that can be used by people.

NOMADIC
Moving from place to place rather than living in one spot.

OFFICIAL LANGUAGE
A language that is approved by the government and is used in law courts, schools, and government offices.

PARLIAMENT
A group of people who meet to decide on a country's laws, oversee its government, and represent the population.

PENINSULA
A piece of land that juts out into the ocean or another body of water.

PLAIN
A large area of flat land.

POPULATION
All the people who live in a particular place.

RAIN FOREST
An area of tall, closely packed trees, found in regions with lots of rain throughout the year.

SAVANNA
An area of grasses dotted with trees, found in hot regions with a dry season and a rainy season.

SPECIES
A group of animals that look similar to each other and can mate with each other.

TECTONIC PLATE
One of the giant, slowly moving slabs of rock that make up Earth's surface.

TEMPERATE
Describing a region of Earth, roughly midway between the Poles and the equator, which does not get either very hot or very cold.

TEXTILE
Cloth made by hand or machine.

TROPICAL
In a region of Earth, around the equator, where it is hot year round.

TUNDRA
An area that is covered by ice for part of the year and is too cold for trees to grow.

VOLCANIC ISLAND
An island that is the peak of an underwater volcano.

VOLCANO
A crack in Earth's surface where molten rock, gas, and ash can erupt.

WETLAND
An area of land where water covers the soil or makes it soggy, either all or part of the time.

Index